"The Ameses' rigorously maintained egalitarian marriage, which spanned the first half of the twentieth century, stands out in Elizabeth Fideler's authoritative telling as an exemplar for our own era of contested gender roles: two remarkable individuals with contrasting temperaments who became 'partners in science' and facilitated each other's passions, from orchids to woman's suffrage and bodily freedom. Fideler has done twenty-first-century readers a tremendous service in resurrecting the lives and times of Blanche and Oakes Ames."

—**Megan Marshall**, Pulitzer Prize-winning author of *Margaret Fuller*

"Blanche and Oakes Ames were descendants of elite families of distinction and notoriety. Elizabeth Fideler documents how they used their family experiences to inform their fifty-year marriage and the goals they set for themselves and shared. Blanche was a social reformer who sought woman's suffrage and birth control; Oakes became an eminent botanist. Blanche illustrated his work with delicate care. Oakes shared his belief in suffrage. Fideler's work demonstrates that they together lived lives that were well lived."

—**Anne Biller Clark**, author of *My Dear Mrs. Ames*

"Elizabeth Fideler has produced an excellent and needed joint-biography of Blanche Ames Ames, artist, suffragist, and reproductive rights advocate, and her husband Oakes Ames, Harvard botanist and authority on orchids. It is a welcome and very readable book on their supportive partnership that spanned half a century. The author has skillfully woven together research and recollections to bring Blanche and Oakes to life. I now know them much better than before."

—**Lisa E. Pearson**, head of the library and archives, Arnold Arboretum Horticultural Library

"Having read all of Oakes Ames's diaries, I believe that Elizabeth Fideler has accurately described and explained the actions and beliefs of Oakes's and Blanche Ames's lives. Oakes stated in one of the diaries that he wanted his children to learn from his diaries. Borderland represented in his words 'a revolution in feelings, ideas, and thoughts.' Elizabeth Fideler has effectively captured the details of this 'revolution.'"

—**Hazel Varella**, secretary, Easton Historical Society

"This is a classic and well-studied account about the life and times of Blanche Ames Ames, her husband Oakes Ames, and their extended families. Elizabeth Fideler sheds light on the accomplishments and insights of these two special individuals who really did change our thoughts regarding the beauty of our surroundings and the desire to bring the world of orchids and the success of the Suffrage Movement to the forefront. The Friends of Borderland thanks Fideler wholeheartedly for bringing their important story to light for all."

—**Norma Urban**, president, Friends of Borderland

Blanche Ames Ames (1878–1969)
and Oakes Ames (1874–1950)

# Blanche Ames Ames
# (1878–1969)
# and
# Oakes Ames
# (1874–1950)

*Cultivating That Mutual Ground*

Elizabeth F. Fideler

RESOURCE *Publications* · Eugene, Oregon

BLANCHE AMES AMES (1878–1969) AND OAKES AMES (1874–1950)
Cultivating That Mutual Ground

Resource Publications
An Imprint of Wipf and Stock Publishers
199 W. 8th Ave., Suite 3
Eugene, OR 97401

www.wipfandstock.com

PAPERBACK ISBN: 978-1-6667-7191-6
HARDCOVER ISBN: 978-1-6667-7192-3
EBOOK ISBN: 978-1-6667-7193-0

05/02/23

# Contents

Blanche Davis b 1934
John P. Davis b 1936
Evelyn Davis b 1942
Ames Davis b 1945

Evelyn Ames b 1910
(& J. P. Davis)

Jessie Ames b 1882

Oakes Ames b 1931
Edward (Ned) Ames b 1933
Olivia Ames b 1937
Joan Ames b 1942

Amyas Ames b 1906
(& Evelyn I. Perkins)

Adelbert Ames Jr b 1880

Ben-Israel Butler b 1855

Paul Butler b 1852

Oliver (Ollie) Ames Jr. b 1945
Angier Ames b 1947
Thomas Ames b 1952

Oliver Ames b 1903
(& Ellen Moseley)

Blanche Ames b 1878
(& Oakes Ames)

Sarah Ames b 1874

Blanche Butler b 1847
(& Adelbert Ames)

Benjamin Franklin Butler b 1818
(& Sarah Hildreth)

John Butler b 1782
(& Charlotte Ellison)

George Ames Plimpton b 1927
Francis T.P. Plimpton Jr. b 1928
Oakes Ames Plimpton b 1933
Sarah G. Plimpton b 1936

Pauline Ames b 1901
(& Francis T.P. Plimpton)

Butler Ames b 1871     Edith Ames b 1873

Charlotte Butler b 1812     Andrew Jackson Butler b 1815

vi

George Ames Plimpton b 1927
Francis T. P. Plimpton Jr. b 1928
Oakes Ames Plimpton b 1933
Sarah G. Plimpton b 1936

Oliver (Ollie) Ames Jr. b 1945
Angier Ames b 1947
Thomas Ames b 1952

Oakes Ames b 1931
Edward (Ned) Ames b 1933
Olivia Ames b 1937
Joan Ames b 1942

Blanche Davis b 1934
John P. Davis b 1936
Evelyn Davis b 1942
Ames Davis b 1945

Pauline Ames b 1901
(& Francis T. P. Plimpton)

Oliver Ames b 1903
(& Ellen Moseley)

Amyas Ames b 1906
(& Evelyn I. Perkins)

Evelyn Ames b 1910
(& J. P. Davis)

William H. Ames b 1861   Evelyn O. Ames b 1863   Anna L. Ames b 1864   **Oakes Ames** b 1874
(& Blanche Ames)
Susan Evelyn Ames b 1867   Lilian Ames b 1870

Oakes Angier Ames b 1829   Frank M. Ames b 1833   Oliver Ames III b 1831
(& Anna Coffin Ray)
Susan E. Ames b 1842   Frederick Lothrop Ames b 1835   Helen A. Ames b 1836

Oakes Ames b 1804
(& Evelina Gilmore)
Oliver Ames II b 1807
(& Sarah Lothrop)

Oliver Ames I "Old Oliver" b 1779
(& Susanna Angier)

vii

# Acknowledgments

M Y HEARTFELT THANKS TO everyone who helped me in some way to tell the story of Blanche Ames Ames and Oakes Ames in book form. I am especially indebted to the many individuals who agreed to be interviewed—all the family members and others with close knowledge of the couple and their many remarkable accomplishments. They not only encouraged me to pursue the biography project, but also provided books, letters, and other documents to aid my research. The Minuteman Library Network and the archivists at the Schlesinger Library/Radcliffe Institute for Advanced Study came through with essential materials. And thanks to Kevin Friend and his BCN Productions we have an excellent documentary film about Borderland.

Paul Clifford, Visitor Service Supervisor at Borderland State Park, conducts an information-packed tour of Borderland, bringing to life the partnership that created it. The Easton Historical Society and Museum and the Friends of Borderland share his enthusiasm and his mission. No doubt everyone associated with Easton's brand new elementary school (named for Blanche Ames Ames) will do the same.

When one's husband is a historian, the bar is set high for scholarship. Special thanks to Paul for encouraging me to reach it.

# Introduction

*"Neither of us alone would have thought of
doing what we have done together."*
—BLANCHE AMES AMES

T HIS IS THE LONG-OVERDUE biography of two unusual people and their
highly productive and enduring partnership. Their story is one of mutual enabling—based on a belief in equality, they cultivated intensively "that
mutual ground," so that his career could prosper and she could take action
even if outside the bounds of what was considered socially acceptable.

Blanche Ames Ames and Oakes Ames had a great deal in common in
addition to joining last names when they got married in 1900. Both were
highly intelligent, curious, hard-working, highly accomplished, strong-
minded, and confident. Both came from socially prominent, affluent
families. They each could claim a father who attained the rank of governor—Blanche's father Adelbert during Reconstruction in Mississippi and
Oakes's father Oliver for a term in Massachusetts. Their respective grand-
fathers had numerous successful business dealings, some of which came
under suspicion. The two families remained tight lipped about the Crédit
Mobilier Scandal in which Oakes's grandfather was implicated and about
the controversial escapades of Blanche's grandfather General Benjamin F.
Butler in the South during and after the Civil War.

Blanche and Oakes had mothers who were strong-willed and who
raised families with six children, all of whom were very well educated at
a time when very few daughters were sent to college. Home and family
life were important to Blanche and Oakes, and they were secure in the
knowledge that they could always rely on family support. At the same time,

they were determined to solve problems for themselves. Individually and as a couple they enjoyed the outdoors, nature, sports, the arts, and travel to distant lands. Both took leadership roles in various organizations and supported causes of local and national importance, not only financially but also in terms of time, talent, and personal commitment.

Nonetheless, their personalities were very different. Blanche was invariably warm, lively, and sociable. Oakes was quiet, shy, and avoided socializing except with his family. His grandchildren—most of whom are in their eighties today—still remember him as a distant, stern, rather formal personage who was not to be disturbed. Children should be seen and not heard, and so on. (This picture of Oakes should be compared with his portrayal in a widely-published 1936 American Academy of Arts and Sciences resolution that made particular mention of Ames's warm, cooperative spirit and of co-workers and colleagues who appreciated his *genial personality,* wise counsel, and generous support.)

Moreover, they did not conform to nineteenth- and early twentieth-century gender roles. Oakes loved Blanche for her feminine attributes *and* for her independence, strength of purpose, and athleticism (considered more "masculine" traits) at a time when women were typically not athletic and were expected to defer to their husbands in all things outside the home and often inside as well. Put another way, women were "expected to look nice and act obedient and let the men do the heavy lifting."[1] In contrast, in a summary of his life for his fiftieth Harvard reunion, Oakes recognized his good fortune in finding a "companionable, gifted wife" who was his "colleague and playfellow" for half a century.[2] Thus, what stands out about Blanche and Oakes Ames is the unflagging support they gave to each other despite dissimilar personalities. Their different ways of being strong might have spelled years of rancor and unhappiness, granddaughter Olivia Ames Hoblitzelle observed, yet the marriage worked because they achieved a balance.

In *Orchids at Christmas*, published jointly by the Ames Family and the Harvard Botanical Museum as a tribute to the couple, Pauline Ames Plimpton remarked on the complementarity of her father's intense interest in botany, particularly orchids, with her mother's artistic talent. She could not think of a more harmonious or devoted couple, each interested in what the other was interested in and sharing it. Even as a young girl, Pauline said,

1. Purnell, Prologue to *A Woman of No Importance,* 2.
2. Plimpton, P. "Coda—Orchids in Bronze," in Ames, *Orchids at Christmas,* 59.

she was aware that their partnership was extraordinary and wished that she would have a marriage like theirs.

> "It goes without saying that she worked with my father in everything he undertook, whether it was illustrating books, being the architect for the house they were building, hearing his lectures, and advising and helping him in his University work . . . . They were a remarkable pair, complementing each other in their capabilities as well as in their natures. My father was rather melancholy, pessimistic, moody—my mother counteracted with her gaiety. He was shy, diffident and reserved, while mother was outgoing, perfectly willing to make a fool of herself and delighting in controversy. My father would vary between being charming and interesting and being quite silent, so that mother would often have to carry the brunt of the conversation at mealtimes."[3]

In the vast land of biography, books about men far outnumber the books about women, and authors tend to choose an already famous or near-famous person to write about, particularly if the subject is female, rather than someone who is quite interesting and accomplished but unknown. The late journalist and storyteller Cokie Roberts expressed the problem succinctly: "One of the reasons I have been writing books about women in history is because other people haven't been. And telling history without talking about one half of the human race seems to me to be an inaccurate way of telling the story."[4]

Blanche Ames Ames was part of women's history for more than half of the twentieth century and deserved to be better known for that and for other reasons. Oakes Ames's contributions to the woman suffrage movement and his extraordinary scientific accomplishments might have received greater recognition had he not avoided the spotlight so successfully. This book is one effort toward correcting those oversights.

Credit is certainly due to historian Anne Biller Clark for a dissertation and book about Blanche's political cartooning on behalf of woman suffrage[5] and to Kevin Friend's fifty-five-minute documentary, "Borderland—The Life and Times of Blanche Ames Ames,"[6] portraying Blanche and Oakes Ames as "two thoroughly original visionaries who fought for fundamental

---

3. Plimpton, P. Introduction to *Jottings of a Harvard Botanist*, 21–23.
4. Roberts, *Cokie: A Life Well Lived*, 189.
5. Clark, *My Dear Mrs. Ames*, PhD diss.; Clark, *My Dear Mrs. Ames*, Peter Lang.
6. Friend, "Borderland—The Life and Times of Blanche Ames Ames."

rights most of us take for granted" and "a Renaissance man and Renaissance woman and then some." However, there has been no attempt to tell the whole story about either of them let alone as a couple in terms of the length and breadth of their partnership, not only in scientific and artistic endeavors, but also in many other ways.

What else has been published about them? Oakes Ames received tributes in several scientific journals, including the American Academy of Arts and Sciences' *Science* and the *Journal of the Arnold Arboretum*, and he has biographical capsules in *International Who's Who, American National Biography*, and *World Biographical Encyclopedia*.[7] Herbarium World devoted a four-part series to his orchid collections and their importance.[8] Blanche Ames Ames earned an entry in *American National Biography* and in *Notable American Women—The Modern Period* where she is indexed under "Arts," "Birth Control," "Feminism," and "Suffrage."[9]

Like Blanche Ames Ames, many of the subjects in *Notable American Women–The Modern Period* came from comfortable backgrounds, from families that encouraged college education for their daughters. They lived "lives that are important in themselves and suggestive as well of the larger social and cultural issues of their time."[10] Many were reformers concerned with public issues, particularly the well-being of women and children, and many were long lived. Where Blanche did not fit the mold, so to speak, was in being married, staying married, and having four children. As the editors point out, "There was more than a little truth to the conventional wisdom that it was difficult for women to have both careers and children, or at least full-time careers and several children . . . those who managed to do so usually had the assistance of servants or relatives."[11] Furthermore, developments in the twentieth century reflected women's changing historical situation, with fewer women limited as their mothers had been to volunteer service as missionaries or as women's club members and more women starting to gain access to the professions. And in this milieu, Blanche could become "a new

7. Motter, "Oakes Ames"; Vassiliki, "Ames, Oakes"; *World Biographical Encyclopedia*, "Oakes Ames, Botanist."

8. Flannery, "Exploring Herbaria and Their Importance."

9. Van Voris, *American National Biography*; Sicherman, *Notable American Women*.

10. Sicherman, Preface to *Notable American Women*, xv.

11. Sicherman, Preface to *Notable American Women*, xvi.

woman" yet remain a generalist, a "gifted amateur . . . who moved easily and successfully among a variety of endeavors."[12]

Blanche Ames Ames was also profiled by Heather Miller in the Harvard Square Library's Digital Library of Unitarian Universalist Biographies, History, Books, and Media as well as by John Simpkin on the Spartacus-Educational web site for teachers and students.[13] Historian James J. Kenneally's research into the story of Blanche Ames Ames's fight for woman suffrage became a pamphlet in which he acknowledged, "This tireless advocate of human freedom and dignity deserves a complete biography."[14]

The writer-narrator of the Borderland documentary, Kate Klise, noted that Blanche Ames Ames was ahead of her times in many ways: "a woman of privilege, a woman of passion, willing to risk her place in society for the causes she believed in . . . . A society woman who was not afraid to shock . . . today we would call her an influencer." And yet, "Her name doesn't appear in most history books. This too is part of her story." For Blanche Ames Ames "paid attention, even when people didn't pay attention to her."[15] As part of her contribution to the documentary, Anne Biller Clark reprised another author's comment about Blanche: "If she was a man, there would be five books already!" Instead, in "an instructive example of how women are written out of history," Blanche was so easily forgotten.[16] As was said of Virginia Hall, an intrepid American spy who organized resistance fighters in 1940s France and became the subject of Sonia Purnell's recent biography, *A Woman of No Importance*,[17] she was anything but.[18]

In addition to emphasizing that attention to the story of Borderland has been wanting, the Borderland documentary called out Blanche's treatment in a *New York Times* obituary that highlighted her marriage to a Harvard professor instead of her own accomplishments: "When Blanche Ames died in 1969, the headline of her obituary identified her as 'Mrs. Oakes

---

12. Sicherman, Preface to *Notable American Women*, xviii.

13. Miller, "Ames, Blanche Ames"; Simpkin, "Blanche Ames" (Suffrage/Cartoonists).

14. Kenneally, "Blanche Ames and Woman Suffrage," 20.

15. Friend, "Borderland—The Life and Times of Blanche Ames Ames."

16. Clark, *My Dear Mrs. Ames*, 156.

17. Purnell, *A Woman of No Importance*.

18. Valentine, "Virginia Hall, The Subject of 'A Woman of No Importance,' Was Anything But." NPR review. "Virginia Hall was one of the earliest Special Operations Executive agents Britain sent into occupied France to stir up resistance against the Nazi/Vichy regime. She laid critical groundwork for organized resistance in southern France and later led a cell herself, carrying on all the while despite the handicap of a prosthetic foot."

Ames, Botanist's Widow', as if her life's work as an artist and activist were an afterthought—or worse, a wasted effort."[19] This was still the custom in obituary writing twenty-six years later when Blanche and Oakes's daughter Pauline Ames Plimpton died in 1995: "As the daughter, wife and mother of famous men, Mrs. Plimpton spent most of her life in the shadow of her father, Oakes Ames, the Harvard botanist; her husband, Francis T. P. Plimpton, the lawyer and diplomat, who died in 1983, and her son, George, the multifaceted editor of *The Paris Review*."[20]

A niece of Blanche and Oakes, Harriet Stevens Robey, wrote a book about the Bay View family compound on the coast of Massachusetts and the several generations of her family that spent their summers there.[21] In the book she devoted an entire section to *bond*, *legacy*, and *trust* and what those words meant to the family, emphasizing that what connected them across generations went well beyond the considerable material wealth and property they managed to acquire and pass along. Were they, and was Oakes's family line as well, part of the nineteenth and twentieth-century elite? Assuredly so. Should Blanche and Oakes Ames be vilified and dismissed on account of their privilege and prominence, or can they be appreciated instead for all they did to advance gender equality and to bring us closer to nature and its bountiful gifts? Now readers can decide for themselves after absorbing the relevant biographical facts.

19. Friend, "Borderland—The Life and Times of Blanche Ames Ames."

20. Thomas Jr., "Pauline A. Plimpton, 93, Author of Works on Famed Relatives."

21. Robey, *Bay View*. Harriet Stevens Robey (1900–1993) was the great-granddaughter of Benjamin F. Butler and Sarah Hildreth Butler, the granddaughter of Adelbert Ames and Blanche Butler Ames, and the daughter of Edith Ames and C. Brooks Stevens, which made her a niece of Blanche and Oakes Ames.

# 1

# Family Background

*Family loyalty, heritage and history*

To know something about Blanche's parents, Adelbert Ames and Blanche Butler Ames, and their strong influence on her, one has to start with her grandparents, the colorful and controversial Benjamin Franklin Butler (1818–1893) and the impressive woman he married in 1844, Sarah Hildreth Butler (1816–1876). Born in New Hampshire, raised in Lowell, Massachusetts, and trained as a lawyer, Ben Butler had military, political, and business careers. "Out of a deprived and fatherless childhood the feisty child grew to be a 'fight-some' man, with every obstacle giving him greater determination to win." And when he met Sarah Hildreth, who was "cultured, intellectual, and a professional actress," he was determined to win her as his wife.[1] They produced two sons, Ben-Israel and Paul, and a daughter called Blanche. Ben-Israel died at age twenty-six. Paul married but had no children. Blanche was the mother of six, including our subject, Blanche Ames Ames.

Promoted to major general in the Union Army during the Civil War and while in command of Fort Monroe, Virginia, Butler refused to return escaped slaves to the Confederacy, arguing successfully that they were "contraband of war." His firm stance in defiance of the Fugitive Slave Act of 1850 not only gave escaped slaves legal protection behind Union lines but also helped to win acceptance of emancipation as an official war goal. However, on the minus side, Butler was later dismissed for battlefield incompetence but not before taking military command of New Orleans. In the role of Occupation Governor there he earned the nickname "The Beast" for ordering

---

1. Robey, *Bay View—A Summer Portrait*, 26.

Confederate women of the city to show respect to Union troops. If they harassed Union soldiers by, for instance, pouring slop buckets on them from upper-story windows, they would be treated like prostitutes. Unfortunately, the Occupation Governor was also associated with war profiteering. The Richmond, Virginia *Examiner* called Butler "the beastliest, bloodiest poltroon and pickpocket the world ever saw."[2] In contrast, pro-Union lyrics that were sung to the tune of "Yankee Doodle" proclaimed, "He helped the poor and snubbed the rich .... Bully for Ben Butler."[3, 4]

During several terms as a congressman from Massachusetts in 1867–1875 and again in 1877–1897, Butler's reputation for grit and intelligence grew. He led the trial of Andrew Johnson in 1868 when the president was under impeachment for vetoing legislation passed by Congress to protect the rights of freedmen. As committee chair of the House Select Committee on Reconstruction in the 41st Congress, he authored the Ku Klux Klan Act (the Civil Rights Act of 1871), and he co-sponsored the Civil Rights Act of 1875 which passed in the 43rd Congress. He was an early supporter of woman suffrage and of the eight-hour workday. He served as the thirty-third governor of Massachusetts in 1883–1884 and ran unsuccessfully for president on the Greenback Party ticket in 1884.

His great-granddaughter Harriet Stevens Robey described him as a remarkable and brilliant man with a prodigious memory who could not tolerate injustice to the underprivileged. As a fledgling lawyer he had worked for better conditions for the mill workers in Lowell and made enemies of the mill owners as a result. He detested slavery and favored suffrage for women.

> "Original, dynamic, picturesque, audacious, and fearless, he had immense vitality. He was a natural politician and an astute if unconventional lawyer; he was 'unsurpassed as a military administrator' but was a poor general in the field. He was a man of many and diversified business interests. He was also well ahead of his time in vision. It has been said that he just missed being a truly great American."[5]

2. Robey, *No Luxury of* Woe, 115.

3. Pierson, "He Helped the Poor and Snubbed the Rich."

4. According to historian Ron Chernow, "Butler had legions of both admirers and enemies. Shrewd and scheming, he was half reformer, half demagogue." Chernow, *Grant*, 371. Also see: Leonard, *Benjamin Franklin Butler—A Noisy, Fearless Life.*

5. Robey, *Bay View*, 19.

His great-granddaughter also described Butler as "obstreperous, abrasive, vituperative, cantankerous, pugnacious, vindictive, and opportunistic . . . . Some questioned his moral fiber. He was admired, even adored, respected, feared, and intensely hated, especially by Southerners, hence the nickname. Yet he was asked by Abraham Lincoln to run as his vice-president in the elections of 1864."[6] Had he accepted the offer, Benjamin F. Butler would have become president when Lincoln was assassinated six weeks after the inauguration.

A small, homely, rotund, but powerful man, Butler had a great nose for promising investments and an uncanny sense of timing when it came to business. His diversified business interests included part ownership of the Middlesex Mills, the Wamesit Power Company, the U.S. Bunting Company, and the U.S. Cartridge Company. The latter firm profited greatly from government contracts for munitions needed during wartime and from supplying shotgun shells, pistol and rifle cartridges to hunters. Indeed, by 1917, U.S. Cartridge had 8,000 employees at its manufacturing plant in Lowell. He also bought up thousands of acres of ranchland in Colorado and New Mexico and a prime strip of waterfront property on Cape Ann near Gloucester, Massachusetts.

General Butler acquired the Cape Ann land in 1863 and, as the story goes, set up a tent on the beach as a make-shift seaside home for himself, his two sons Paul and Ben-Israel, and their tutor, while his wife and daughter lived in a farmhouse nearby. One year later he was again living in a tent, this time as major general in command of the Union Army of the James on the battlefield in Virginia. In the summer of 1865 he returned to Cape Ann and decided to build a proper residence to be called "The Homestead" higher up on the granite hillside. The granite for the house came from a Cape Ann quarry that Butler had purchased with his business partner, a Civil War colonel named Jonas French. The family compound that grew around The Homestead was known as "Bay View."

The general's son Paul loved sailing at Bay View and yachting (he inherited the racing yacht *America* from his father). Paul's older brother Ben-Israel, a West Point graduate, was about to go into business with General Butler when he died of Bright's disease in 1881. Thus, after the general passed on in 1893, it was Paul who took over his father's businesses. "Wise, generous, and far-sighted," Harriet Stevens Robey enthused, Paul Butler (who had no children of his own) left all his assets in trust to his sister

6. Robey, *Bay View*, 19–20.

Blanche's children and their issue. The Colorado and New Mexico ranches and fifty-eight acres of Bay View are held in family trusts to this day.

Robey's book about Bay View describes generations of children spending the summer by the water playing games, exploring, cliff climbing, swimming, fishing, sailing, reading, picnicking, making sand castles, and—until caught in the act—getting into mischief. "All the time we were growing up we lived the sea, were part of it . . . the changes of the tides were in our bones."[7] Author Robey also realized as she grew older what an isolated paradise Bay View was, set apart from the village and its inhabitants and restricting their access to the shoreline.[8] And, at the same time, she wondered how much Bay View and its clannishness was a factor in shaping the children's personalities.[9]

We turn next to Benjamin and Sarah Butler's daughter, Blanche Butler Ames (1847–1939), The collected letters of Blanche Butler Ames, her *Chronicles from the Nineteenth Century*,[10] record the story of her marriage to Adelbert Ames (1835–1933), a Civil War general of far greater distinction than her father, and of their family life. "There is a heroic quality about the two; one can call it stature, or courage, or idealism, or loyalty, or patience, or self-abnegation, or all of them together . . . . What the *Chronicles* amount to is, quite simply, a sixty-three-year love story of two fine people. And whether one was more dominant than the other is unimportant at this point in the face of the endurance and integrity of each."[11] In addition to her genealogical interests, Blanche Butler Ames excelled at gardening and sculpture and made sure that all of her children—Butler, Edith, Sarah, Blanche, Adelbert Jr., and Jessie—were college educated.

The "clannishness" fostered at Bay View and in Lowell was based on family bonds, legacy, and trust. In her Foreword to *Bay View*, Robey explained that she initially saw the book as a chronicle, a compilation of memories of Bay View and the clan that summered there, "bound by invisible ties of kinship and inheritance."[12] However, challenged by a question from a great-niece about how and why the Ames women were *strong*, the author pivoted toward "almost a sociological study of the Butler Hildreth

7. Robey, *Bay View*, 219.

8. Robey, *Bay View*, 180.

9. Robey, *Bay View*, 8.

10. Ames, Blanche Butler. *Chronicles from the Nineteenth Century*.

11. Robey, *Bay View*, 148.

12. Robey, *Bay View*, x.

Ames inheritance."[13] In a later book written when Robey was ninety-two, she added *stoicism* to the list of family characteristics. Stoicism became the family's watchword, being preferable to talking about their feelings.

The title of the later book, *No Luxury of Woe*, came from one of Benjamin Butler's letters to his wife Sarah in which he acknowledged that she was not one to luxuriate in woe.[14] Sarah made sure her adolescent daughter Blanche got the message. When Blanche Butler was sent to the Academy of the Visitation in Washington, D.C. where students made fun of her Yankee accent, she wrote home to her mother with complaints about her schoolmates, her dresses, and her various physical ailments. Sarah admonished Blanche for complaining and reminded her that she was expected to become a highly educated and accomplished woman, not one who indulged in idleness. Contrary to then-prevailing norms of womanhood that encouraged passivity and dependence on others, Benjamin and Sarah Butler nurtured their daughter's artistic inclinations and expected her to think for herself.

No wonder that when Blanche Butler agreed to marry Adelbert "Del" Ames, it was on the condition that "obey" be omitted from their marriage vows. Fortunately, Del believed in love, not obedience. He and Blanche were married in 1870 and started their family a year later. And, while serving as Reconstruction governor and senator from Mississippi, he listened to his wife's advice about his public speeches and attempts at reform, Blanche having often witnessed her father's oratory during important debates (including in 1868 during the impeachment trial of President Andrew Johnson) and his legislative accomplishments as chair of the House Committee on Reconstruction.

Blanche Butler Ames's first child, Butler, was terribly demanding and often mean, especially to his little sister Edith. He grew up to be much like his grandfather, General Butler, a brash fellow who expected to get his way. The story of Butler Ames and the Villa Balbianello on Lake Como in Italy illustrates the point and is an unusual part of the family lore.[15] The Villa Balbianello was from 1919 to 1974 the vacation home of Butler Ames and chosen family members—he banned his sister Edith when she criticized his behavior, a vestige of the old sibling rivalry—and is still today one of the most beautiful properties on a lake of singular beauty. It was first the site of Pliny the Younger's villa, for a time a cardinal's retreat, then the property of

13. Robey, *Bay View*, ix.
14. Robey, *No Luxury of Woe*.
15. Plimpton, O., *Butler Ames and the Villa Balbianello*.

Gian Martino Arconati Visconti and his wife Marie Peyrat, the Marquesa. How did an American family come into the possession of a magnificent villa on Lake Como in Italy? It was all the doing of Butler Ames, who followed in the footsteps of his father and grandfather as a military man (West Point graduate, lieutenant colonel in the Spanish-American War, major general in the Massachusetts National Guard), politician (congressman from Massachusetts 5th Congressional District), and businessman (U.S. Cartridge Co. and Heinze Electric Co. in Lowell, Massachusetts).

Butler Ames spotted the villa on a trip to Italy in 1911 and was determined to purchase the property and its furnishings, paintings, and library from the fabulously wealthy Marquesa, who lived in France and other locations. For the next eight years, she refused all offers, no matter how large, from Butler Ames and other interested parties, preferring to leave the place unoccupied. Geopolitical realignments after World War I worked in Ames's favor and the villa was finally his. He and his wife Fifi stayed there every summer until Butler Ames died in 1954, leaving the villa in trust for twenty years to the four children of his favorite sister, Blanche Ames Ames. Pauline Ames Plimpton[16] and her husband Francis T. P. Plimpton used it the most, hosting visits from family members and from friends like Jackie Onassis and Adlai Stevenson. After 1974, a Count Guido Monzinio owned the estate for the next fourteen years and upon his death bequeathed it to the care of the Italian Heritage Fund.

Perhaps Butler Ames's personality was shaped by his early years with an overly indulgent mother and a father who was largely absent due to military and political obligations. Adelbert Ames came from Maine, graduated from West Point in 1861, and was off to the Civil War. He received the Congressional Medal of Honor for valor in the Battle of Bull Run, held Union Army brigade and division commands (leading, for example, the Twentieth Maine Voluntary Infantry Regiment before Lt. Col. Joshua L. Chamberlain was given command and gained fame at the Battle of Gettysburg) and attained the rank of major general. He was appointed Provisional Governor of Mississippi in 1868, represented the state in the U.S. Senate from 1870–1873, and served as governor of the state from 1873–1876. His experience in the South was so fraught with peril that his wife remained at home with the children in Lowell except for the briefest of obligatory visits. Conditions in Mississippi during Reconstruction were terrible, Blanche Butler Ames wrote

16. Like his mother Pauline Ames Plimpton, great-grandmother Blanche Butler Ames, and cousin Harriet Stevens Robey, Oakes Ames Plimpton collected family history.

to her mother Sarah from Jackson, Mississippi. The governor faced a reign of terror, fraudulent elections, and Southern Democrats clamoring for his impeachment—white supremacists who vilified the governor for extending rights to freed slaves and appointing them to office. If they could not succeed in impeaching him, Blanche feared they would not hesitate to assassinate him. And, she felt, nobody in the North realized how dire the conditions really were. In a "darkly prophetic" letter to his wife, the governor had "previewed the nearly century-long Jim Crow system that would cast blacks back into a state of involuntary servitude to southern whites."[17]

Forced to resign, Governor Adelbert Ames testified under oath for three days before a congressional committee charged with investigating the situation in Mississippi and was completely vindicated. (That did not stop John F. Kennedy from besmirching Governor Ames's name years later in *Profiles in Courage*. As discussed in chapter 10, the governor's outraged daughter Blanche, then in her eighties, researched and wrote a book of nearly 600 pages about her father to set the record straight.[18]) After leaving office, Adelbert Ames worked in the family flour-milling business in Northfield, Minnesota, before returning to New England and his family. After so many pain-filled years, he was ready to pass leisurely summer days in The Homestead at Bay View that his wife had inherited from her father and winter months in Ormond, Florida. He later returned briefly to military service as a brigadier general in the Spanish-American War. When Adelbert Ames died in 1933, he was at age ninety-eight the last surviving general of the Civil War who held rank in the regular U.S. Army.

As to the matriarchy of the Ames women, part three of Robey's *Bay View* shed light on how it functioned by means of a combination of masculine intelligence and a feminine sensibility, "partly inherited, partly learned through precept and/or indoctrination." Those quite different qualities posed a problem for the Ames women: how to embody the feminine role as a well-bred, dignified lady when determined "to analyze, to control, to master and manage. We are problem-solving reorganization women," Robey asserted.[19] Mothers would give sons their independence much earlier than daughters; daughters were admonished to guard their virtue. Mothers kept daughters close to them by *giving and giving*, only expecting in return love and upholding the standards of the family. In this way,

17. Chernow, *Grant*, 815.

18. Ames, B. *Adelbert Ames, 1835–1933: General, Senator, Governor.*

19. Robey, *Bay View*, 349.

Blanche Butler Ames and her four daughters remained exceptionally close. And when Blanche Butler Ames at age ninety-two insisted on a lethal dose that would end her life and got her way on December 26, 1939, daughters Edith, Sarah, Blanche, and Jessie were with her.

Author Robey wondered how much the taboos on premarital sex and depiction of marital sex as a "duty" affected daughters' adult sexuality. And how much did the early training in being practical, knowing, and realistic shut the door to creativity and originality? Robey noted the family's lack of true poets, deeply original artists, and creative writers. Evelyn Perkins Ames, the first wife of her cousin Amyas Ames, was a writer and poet, but "Evvie" had not been raised among Ames women. Aunt Blanche Ames Ames (who was) was every bit an artist, whether or not she was a deeply original one, Robey opined. It seemed "that the need for eternal watchfulness of self and eternal drawing on inner strength, with its denial of weakness, has a part in negating the tremendous potential for creativity among the Ames women. A few have found it, a few have liberated psyches, but even then there are 'imprinted' those first early associations. Control yourself indomitably and you control your world."[20] This mantra extended to staying one jump ahead of one's husband during decision-making discussions, appearing to cater to his preferences while questioning their merits.

Robey cited other characteristics of Ames women that describe Blanche Ames Ames nicely—her need to love and be loved; her occasional displays of whimsy, spontaneity, and unconventionality (behaviors so distasteful to her mother-in-law, Anna C. Ames!); and her disinterest in showing off via social climbing or lavishness of décor. In addition, Blanche was not the "touching, caressing, hugging kind." And her response to being taken advantage of or being betrayed was outrage and often a lawsuit.[21]

Harriet Robey admired and adored her Aunt Blanche, who vacationed at Bay View in the former life-saving station after renovations and improvements to the old building—water was piped in, a studio was added—to make it habitable for the growing Ames family and suitable for her art projects. The Ames cousins were Harriet's favorites: Pauline was named for Blanche's brother Paul Butler; Oliver was named for Oakes's father, the governor; Amyas was an old English spelling of Ames; and Evelyn was named for Oakes's sister. Aunt Blanche was, among other things, an imaginative storyteller who could be funny and incisive and a wonderful teacher. She taught

20. Robey, *Bay View*, 353.
21. Robey, *Bay View*, 355.

the children, not only her own, how to model sea creatures in plasticene and to produce a cast of the original. In Robey's estimation, Aunt Blanche was the most creative of the four talented sisters, for as Uncle Oakes grew famous in the field of botany for his dedication to orchids, Blanche became his illustrator. "Her originality and sense of shape and form flowed through the perfection of her technique and accuracy in reproduction to make each drawing a thing of beauty."[22] Despite family tradition, however, after 1918 Blanche and Oakes stopped going to Bay View. It was less of an attraction once they had Borderland, and feeling like an "out-law" made going to the family compound a chore for Oakes.

It is curious that Robey's *Bay View* omitted the painful part of Blanche's artistic career that involved her younger brother Adelbert Ames Jr. (1880–1955). Perhaps it was stoicism that kept Aunt Blanche from talking about it, leaving her unenlightened niece to misrepresent her Uncle Del as "one of the real heroes of our family" although he was seldom at Bay View and in fact Harriet hardly knew him.[23] Apparently, she and Uncle Del had one conversation in 1938 that was significant for Robey because he helped her to "find herself" by recommending that she see a psychoanalyst about her feelings of depression and struggles to deal with her (unexplained) "situation." Uncle Del also talked extensively to his niece about himself, his career, and socializing after graduating from Harvard Law School in 1906, and how he radically changed his life. Robey admitted that she was "not too clear just what happened next."[24] What is striking in the *Bay View* pages that followed is the absence of his sister Blanche from Del's story, despite the very generous support she gave her brother when the rest of the family turned away from him, his use of Blanche's studio at Borderland, and the work they did together on the system of color theory, for which he took sole credit. Uncle Del gave his niece to believe that he had *by his own bootstraps* set himself free. Had Blanche and Oakes told her about *their* experience with Del, Harriet would have realized she was badly mistaken in describing her uncle as modest and self-effacing.

A far more objective depiction of the brother-sister story came from art historian and professor Roy R. Behrens. His essay reviewed Blanche's artistic and scientific collaboration with her brother Adelbert Jr. and Oakes's

22. Robey, *Bay View*, 167.
23. Robey, *Bay View*, 303.
24. Robey, *Bay View*, 305.

reaction to it.[25] When Del unexpectedly did an about-face, gave up law, and decided to embark on a career as a professional artist, family and friends were shocked. His sister Blanche was the only one who stood by him and helped with financial support. She also shared her studio space with Del and helped him learn how to paint. Blanche shared the experience gained in the ten years following her marriage to Oakes when she had been illustrating his publications about orchids, first in watercolor, then using copperplate etchings. For pen and ink drawings she used a camera lucida— literally "light chamber," a light, portable optical device facilitating the accurate drawing of an object—and a combination microscope and camera. Del became familiar with her equipment as well.

Between 1910 and 1913 Blanche and Del collaborated on the study of color, perspective, and other aspects of representational art. By 1912 they had developed a complex color notation system. The Ames System was comprised of "approximately 3,300 variations of hues, values, and intensities, precisely computed and painted on cards, then labeled with a code that matched the same number and variety of tubes of paint."[26] Working together on perspective in drawing or painting, they began to investigate the science of perception, specifically the different advantages of binocular and monocular vision when making art. This came about when Blanche used the "color swatch" system she and Del had created to paint an elm tree that was on the grounds at Borderland. Though the painting was "wonderfully detailed," they thought it "did not successfully convey the illusion of depth," and so they began to research binocular and peripheral vision using two cameras to replicate human vision.[27] They also built a grid-divided drawing frame through which the artist could view a model or subject matter when preparing to draw or photograph it.

Behrens's examination of Oakes's diary entries for this time revealed stirrings of jealousy provoked by Blanche devoting so much time to her brother. By 1913 tensions had abated, however. Del was doing research on optical physiology at Clark University and then at Dartmouth, and Blanche had jumped into suffrage work, hosting planning meetings and lectures in the spacious library at Borderland and drawing a series of political cartoons seeking support for passage of an amendment to the state constitution in

25. Behrens, "The Artistic and Scientific Collaboration."
26. Behrens, "The Artistic and Scientific Collaboration," 49–50.
27. Dempsey, "Women Artists: An Untold Story," 10–11.

1915. Oakes pitched in to help as chair of the campaign committee of the Men's League for Woman Suffrage. (See chapter 5.)

Time passed. Then, in the 1920s, Del began to publish articles about the optical research he was doing, listing himself as *sole* author or as co-author with a Dartmouth colleague, and without crediting his sister's contributions to the work. Oakes, a professor and much-published scholar familiar with the customs of scientific work and academic journals, undertook the delicate task of getting his wife to see how her brother refused to acknowledge making extensive use of her knowledge and experience and failed to give her joint authorship. For some time he had been trying to warn Blanche about Del's underhandedness, but she, believing her brother incapable of disloyalty and foul play, stubbornly refused to concede the point. Family loyalty was again coming between Blanche and Oakes as it had in the earlier years of their marriage.

Oakes tried another tack, meeting with his brother-in law Del in an attempt to get him to mend his ways. It was only after "considerable friction" between herself and her husband that Blanche realized Oakes was defending her interests and finally came around to believing he was right in his criticism.[28] Although Del continued his research and Blanche went on with her art and many other accomplishments, the dispute with Del over authorship left a very unpleasant taste. As Behrens concluded, "While their relationship was cordial in later years, it appears that their closeness was never restored."[29]

Although Harriet Robey was completely unaware of Del's breach of trust, she did put a lot of stock in family probity and dependability. To conclude her story of Bay View, Robey revisited the legacy of *trust* within the clan, by which she referred to two things—trust in a figurative sense meaning the physical and emotional experience, the freedom to grow into independence for all who were lucky enough to be there; and trust literally meaning the legal arrangements binding the generations, the Paul Butler Trust and the Beach Realty Trust. Those trusts were obviously legal documents, yet they also stood for more than monetary or property assets. They represented strong family loyalty, heritage and history. "We seem to have deep resources that are not fostered by faith or dependency but lie instead in ourselves and in our traditions," she observed.[30] Moreover, she claimed, those resources,

28. Behrens, "The Artistic and Scientific Collaboration," 52.

29. Behrens, "The Artistic and Scientific Collaboration," 53.

30. Robey, *Bay View*, 340.

whether financial or personal, were achieved through self-reliance—again, the "bootstraps" metaphor—and not by religion. Aside from Evelyn Ames Davis' husband (son-in-law of Blanche and Oakes) who left a law practice to attend theological seminary and become an Episcopal minister, Ames family members were not religiously observant.

Reading *Bay View* and *No Luxury of Woe*, one cannot help noticing that their author was up front about some problems, such as serious physical illnesses that struck adults and children in the extended family, but either did not know or did not want to know about or do more than hint at other behaviors that can beset any family, such as sibling disagreements, marital stress, divorce, alcohol or substance abuse, premarital sex, untraditional sexual proclivities, financial troubles, and mental illness. Instead, she wrote about summertime activities at the seashore, loving fathers, devoted mothers, and family traits like staunchness, patience, self-denial, uncomplaining acceptance of suffering, and loyalty. Events in the wider world that were outside the book's focus were similarly neglected. In contrast, descriptions of the family's various summer residences and their outings in the yacht *America* went on and on.

Whereas innumerable pages have been written about Blanche Ames Ames's ancestors, there is no comparable chronicle of Oakes Ames's ancestry, merely brief biographical sketches of family members who are often referred to as the "Shovel Ameses." Although the descriptor is anything but glamorous, any reader who underestimates its significance would be greatly mistaken. Oakes great-grandfather, known as "Old Oliver," was born in 1779 and was manufacturing shovels in North Easton, Massachusetts by 1804. Business prospered at the Ames Shovel and Tool Company (later renamed Ames and Sons), shovels being in great demand during the Gold Rush in California and Australia, throughout the Civil War, and for building the Transcontinental Railroad. Old Oliver and his wife Susanna had two sons, Oakes (1804–1873) and Oliver II (1807–1877), who took over the shovel business. This Oakes (the grandfather of our subject, Oakes) had four children with his wife Evelina, one of whom was Oliver Ames III (the father of our Oakes). In addition to his business interests, Oakes was successful in politics, representing the 2nd District of Massachusetts in Congress from 1863–1873.

Congressman Oakes Ames was a member of the House Committee on Railroads. Before serving in Congress, in 1862 he had invested $200,000 in the construction of the Central Pacific stretch of tracks being built eastward from San Francisco. Notably, the year 1862 was when President Lincoln signed the Pacific Railway Act, authorizing a Union Pacific line to meet up with the Central Pacific and bring the nation closer together economically and politically via the first transcontinental line in the United States.[31] By 1865, when work on the Union Pacific was behind schedule and foundering under the direction of Thomas C. Durant, President Lincoln asked Congressman Oakes Ames to oversee completion of the line westward from the Missouri River. It would make his reputation, the president insisted. Indeed, the people of Ames, Iowa named their town after him. By 1866 Oakes's brother Oliver had signed on as president of the Union Pacific and the two men raised the funds needed to get the job done.

Here we will digress from the laudatory family story to consider a definitive account of the Union Pacific's birth by historian Maury Klein with its more sobering details.[32] Oakes and Oliver were very different people and they ended up in quite different positions. As described by Klein, the older brother Oakes was a tower of strength, but he tended to be impetuous and careless of details. Oliver was more studious and reflective than Oakes, and while he became president of the Union Pacific after the ouster of Durant, he lacked the temperament to deal with its constant challenges.

Aside from the difficulties of construction across mountains and desert, the most serious challenge was the Crédit Mobilier scheme that captivated the country both during the Grant Administration and for many years thereafter. Crédit Mobilier was created in 1864 to help finance the building of the railroad, as the federal government's subsidy was inadequate from the start and subject to political infighting. Management, involving two separate boards, each controlled by competing pools of investors, was extremely complex. Oakes, as a congressman and a member of the House Committee on Railroads, was particularly vulnerable to political charges of conflict of interest, real or impugned.

The Ames brothers, who had large fortunes built on ownership of the Ames Shovel and Tool Company, provided funds and raised money from other investors to help cover the railroad's debts. All of this was done under highly speculative and uncertain conditions: repayment of the investments was based on the sale of the land lying within the railroad

31. U.S. House of Representatives, "History, Art & Archives."

32. Klein, *Union Pacific, Vol. I.* As summarized for Elizabeth Fideler by Edward (Ned) Ames.

corridor designated by Congress, rather than on the profits earned from its still minimal operations.

Klein's narrative criticized the poor management abilities of the Ames brothers for much of what followed. He described in particular their weakness in dealing with Thomas C. Durant, who in addition to being an early investor from New York had become president of the Union Pacific. Durant was intent on taking profits from the construction of the railroad while Oliver and Oakes were content to wait for operating profits once the road was up and running. From the beginning, Klein explained, Durant used complex maneuvers to strip profits and the brothers were unable to stop him. There were endless arguments over the route for the tracks, debates that were both politically and financially charged. Eventually, the Ames brothers and their investor friends achieved majority stock positions, the corrupt Durant lost his position, and Oliver became president of the Union Pacific.

In 1872, the press published reports exposing all sorts of irregularities in the enterprise. A charge was brought in Congress that Oakes had offered shares of stock to members of Congress at less than their par value, allegedly in attempts to bribe members to increase their support for the railroad. Oakes denied the charges, which were never proven, but his involvement in the companies' financial dealings made it difficult for him to separate himself from the charges entirely and resulted in his censure by Congress.

While the building of the Transcontinental Railroad proved to be a primary factor in the economic development of the nation, it inevitably allowed the spread of environmental degradation westward as settlers converted the prairie to tilled farmland and pastureland. Klein described the Union Pacific as the "queen on the chessboard of economic development." Branch lines and spurs were built to procure iron and coal deposits that were needed for its operations and to obtain other lucrative minerals. Extraction of ores was largely unregulated and the processes used resulted in toxic runoff, the impact of which affects environmental quality to this day, particularly in Wyoming, Colorado and Utah. Railroad operations required enormous amounts of both coal and water, the latter being an increasingly scarce resource as the tracks moved west across mountain and desert terrain. In addition, the wooden ties on which the rails were laid were in extremely short supply, and forests were stripped across the country to obtain timbers.

By the time completion of the Transcontinental Railroad could be celebrated at Promontory Summit in Utah Territory in 1869, the feat had come at great cost to the Central Pacific's workforce that was made up almost entirely of Chinese immigrants and at even greater cost to Native Americans living across the Plains and into the Rocky Mountains. When they resisted the railroad's progress by attacking surveyors and construction crews, the U.S. Army was called on to eliminate the tribes or at least to drive them off their ancestral lands. While the defeat of the Native American tribes is part of a much larger story, the loss of the prairie grasslands with their bison herds, a process that was hastened by the building of the railroads, had contributed by the early 1880s to the end of the Native American culture as it once existed.[33]

President Lincoln was correct in saying that the Union Pacific would make Oakes's reputation, but he did not foresee that it would be a tarnished reputation. Sensing the immense profits to be had from building the railroad—construction being more profitable than usage at the time—members of Congress clamored to buy shares of company stock. The aforementioned Crédit Mobilier Scandal resulted in Congressman Oakes Ames being investigated for having sold shares at bargain rates to some dozen House colleagues, including Schuyler Colfax, then-speaker of the House of Representatives who, in 1869, became the 17th vice president of the United States, and senator Henry Wilson, who was the 18th vice president from 1873–1875 (both serving in the Grant administration). The other congressmen having dumped their shares before the investigation, only Representative James Brooks of New York (also a director for the Union Pacific) profited. On February 27, 1873, the House censured Congressmen Ames and Brooks for using their political influence for personal financial gain. In another intriguing crossover between the two political families under study, Benjamin F. Butler was the lawyer who mounted Oakes Ames's successful defense. Congressman Ames was acquitted of the most damaging charges of fraud and bribery, but he died soon afterward.

Oakes Ames's son Oliver III (1831–1895) was the next head of the pick and shovel business. Oliver III and his wife Anna (1839–1917) had a large family—William, Evelina, Anna, Susan, Lilian, and our orchid-loving Oakes, last-born in their brood of six. In addition to their residence called "The Homestead" (what else?) on Oliver Street in North Easton, they built an elegant mansion at 355 Commonwealth Avenue in Boston

33. Conclusions by Edward (Ned) Ames, based on Klein, *Union Pacific, Vol. I.*

in time for the 1883–1884 winter season. Said to have cost $100,000, 355 Commonwealth was, according to Bainbridge Bunting's *Houses of Boston's Back Bay*,[34] the first of the Boston chateaux. These were very large houses "deriving inspiration from the sixteenth century chateaux of the Loire Valley. The most interesting feature of the exterior is the wealth of exquisitely carved brownstone relief. The delicate pilaster arabesques and friezes filled with floral forms contrast with crisp rectangular architectural forms. One notes especially the panels of relief above the first story windows. Here putti intertwine with plant forms and engage in various homey activities relating to the use of the corresponding room inside: eating, playing musical instruments, conversing, and so forth."[35]

Over and above his business affairs, Oliver III was also active in Republican politics and served in 1883 as lieutenant governor of Massachusetts under Democrat Benjamin F. Butler (another crossover!) and then served three terms as governor of the Commonwealth between 1887–1890. As governor, Oliver Ames's public life was primarily devoted to clearing the name of his late father Oakes Ames, still under a cloud for his role in the Crédit Mobilier Scandal, as explained above. In addition, his tenure in office was marked by a divide within the Commonwealth over the growing temperance movement.[36] Governor Ames was executor of his father's estate and took over many of his business interests. He was a patron of sports and the arts. He owned Booth's Theater in New York City and raised funds to send members of the Boston Athletic Association to the 1896 Summer Olympics.

The governor was a major philanthropist, especially in his hometown of North Easton. With his cousins Frederick Lothrop Ames and Helen Angier Ames, Oliver Ames financed the construction of many projects designed by architect Henry Hobson Richardson and landscape designer Frederick Law Olmsted in North Easton, Massachusetts, including Oakes Ames Memorial Hall in 1881, the Ames Free Library, the Old Colony Railroad station (more recently the home of the Easton Historical Society and Museum), and the gatehouse and farmhouse on the John Ames estate. The cousins donated generously to the Oliver Ames High School and the Unitarian Church in the town. The site of these properties is now the H. H. Richardson Historic District of North Easton, a National Historic

34. Bunting, *Houses of Boston's Back Bay*.
35. Back Bay Houses, www.backbayhouses.org.
36. www.en.wikipedia.org.

Landmark District. (H. H. Richardson also designed the Union Pacific Railroad's monument to Oakes and Oliver Ames near the town of Sherman, Wyoming, which is graced with *bas relief* medallions of the brothers on the sides, sculptures designed by Augustus Saint-Gaudens.)

And now for the penultimate crossover between the two families: Oakes met Butler Ames when he joined a militia battery at the time of the Spanish-American War. And through their friendship, Oakes met Butler's younger sister Blanche, a Smith College student, whom he would marry in 1900. "I decided at once that she was worth cultivation. The rest is history."[37]

---

37. Ames, O., *Jottings of a Harvard Botanist*, 66.

# 2

# Courtship, Marriage, and Early Days

*"They were a remarkable pair, complementing each other,*
*not only in their capabilities but in their natures."*
—PAULINE AMES PLIMPTON

OAKES WAS BORN IN North Easton, Massachusetts on September 26, 1874, the youngest of Oliver and Anna C. Ames's six children. His mother Anna was particularly attached to him. He spent the summer in North Easton and attended public school there in the fall months before the family removed to Boston for the winter. In the Boston House at 355 Commonwealth Avenue (which he and Blanche later owned), he stocked up on "youthful adventures on a glorious street." Oakes had less to say in his personal journal about attending the private Hopkinson's School for Boys than about the corner drugstore's prescription department where he liked to hang out. It was there that he picked up Latin and pharmacological terms that proved useful later on when he became an instructor of economic botany at Harvard (the study of the ways humans use plants for food, medicines, and commerce). Oakes admitted that he did not shine at school and needed to be tutored in algebra and chemistry and Latin composition over the summer of 1894 in order to be accepted to Harvard. He also admitted that he was "astonishingly lazy" unless he had a deep interest in something, and then he would put his "full power" to the task.[1]

Oakes devoted several pages in *Jottings* to explaining his choice of a career in botany rather than in manufacturing or politics or the banking business—which was on offer—thus breaking with family tradition. The direction he chose to pursue was a felicitous combination of nature and

1. Ames, O., *Jottings of a Harvard Botanist*, 51–52.

nurture, assisted by the family's deep pockets and personal connections. His father, who had become quite sickly after his political career ended, enjoyed outings with his nursing attendant to pick roadside wildflowers. Since the Ames's gardener could not name many of them, his father purchased *Gray's Manual of Botany*, sixth edition, and a book about wildflowers and Oakes was drawn into helping with identifications. Up to this point, he could only recognize dandelions, violets, buttercups, daisies, roses, and pond lilies. The teenager began making excursions on his own into the fields and woods around North Easton in a search for new flowers that he brought home in a tin biscuit box. His father, who approved of this nascent interest much more than his son's passion for football, replaced an old greenhouse with new greenhouses that could accommodate their growing collection of water lilies and orchids and hired a new and very knowledgeable gardener who taught Oakes how to dry and classify plants correctly.

Oakes was fascinated, and his collection of orchids grew by leaps and bounds. Nathaniel Lord Britton, the director of the New York Botanical Garden, helped to nurture his interest in orchidology.[2] This led to forming a herbarium (a place to store his collection of dried, labeled, and numbered plant specimens) and acquiring the classics of orchidology for his library. Botany studies at Harvard and trips to see orchid holdings at the Royal Botanic Gardens at Kew in southwest London followed. "Orchids dominated my life and to pry into their meaning was a compelling pastime," he said. While he did credit Harvard professor Charles Townsend Copeland for turning him on to English literature and praised Charles Eliot Norton's lectures on the fine arts, it was George Lincoln Goodale in Botany I who rose above the rest.[3]

Oakes nearly did not graduate with his class, however, owing to a "bombshell." A failed test in Latin 10 put him out of the course and a half-credit short of finishing his undergraduate degree. Luckily, the dean made an exception and allowed Oakes to earn the necessary credit by doing laboratory research under the supervision of botany professor W. G. Farlow. Based on this personal experience, over the many years he worked with students at Harvard Oakes always believed that rules in special cases were meant to be broken.

Oakes graduated from Harvard with a bachelor's degree in botany in 1898, earned a master's in botany in 1899 under Professor Goodale, and

2. Harvard University, www.hollisarchives.lib.harvard.edu.
3. Ames, O., *Jottings of a Harvard Botanist*, 53–56.

married Blanche Ames the next year on May 15. In short order he established the Ames Botanical Laboratory, began teaching botany at Harvard, and produced the first two of his seven-volume series of *Orchidaceae*.[4] Fascicle I (a part of a book published as a separate section) with illustrations and studies of the family *Orchidaceae* was credited to the Ames Botanical Laboratory in North Easton, Massachusetts in 1905 and was reviewed in the journal *Science*.[5] The reviewer deemed it "an ambitious undertaking" that reminded him of similar botanical projects published in the previous half century by such luminaries as Gray, Goodale, Eaton, and Sargent. The plates were beautifully drawn (not yet by Blanche), the anatomical details illustrated "with great clearness and fidelity." The reviewer was also reassured to learn that the author's multi-volume undertaking did not depend on popular support and would therefore have a good chance of enjoying "a reasonable permanence." (As it most certainly did. Owing to Oakes's scholarship and Blanche's drawings, the seven-volume treatise on orchids, praised as the best researched and classified of all the large plant families, is still used today.[6]) Oakes was beginning to be acknowledged as an expert in his field; proof of this came in an invitation to contribute the section on orchids to the seventh edition of *Gray's Manual of Botany*, to write for other scientific publications, and to classify the Philippine orchids.

Blanche was born to Adelbert and Blanche Butler Ames in Lowell, Massachusetts on February 18, 1878, the fourth of their six children. She graduated from the Rogers Hall School in Lowell in 1895 and earned her bachelor's degree in art history and a diploma in studio art from Smith College in 1899. Just as Sarah and her daughter Blanche had exchanged letters when they were apart, Blanche corresponded often with her daughters when they were away at college and the two Blanches stayed connected by sharing feelings, news, and, from the elder Blanche, motherly advice and reassurance when Blanche was at Smith and for many years thereafter.

Compared to Bryn Mawr where Blanche's older sisters went, Smith gave students an unusual degree of social freedom and encouraged their active participation in sports and other campus activities as well as in the town's musical and theatrical programs and in outings to the countryside.[7] And, of even greater importance, Smith permitted female students

4. Ames, O., *Orchidaceae*.
5. Bessey, "Orchidaceae," 786–787.
6. Miller, "Ames, Blanche Ames."
7. Clark, *My Dear Mrs. Ames*, 50.

to attend its art school where Blanche got the training in drawing, paint-ing, and sculpture she called on for the rest of her life. At Smith, Blanche excelled in basketball and campus politics. Already a "confirmed suffrag-ist" by 1899, her patience was sorely tried when she had to represent the *anti*-suffrage position in a history class debate.[8] This proved to be very good preparation for the many battles to come during her long lifetime (and how clever that history professor was!), as was her election to the position of senior class president. Like her grandmother Sarah Hildreth Butler, who had been a popular Shakespearean actress before her mar-riage, Blanche could hold an audience, whether she was debating women's rights or delivering the commencement address. In her speech for the Ivy Exercises on June 19, 1899 (attended by none other than President Wil-liam McKinley), Blanche declared: "We feel that we are most fortunate to live in an age that—more than any other—makes it possible for women to attain the best and truest development in life."[9]

As she turned twenty-one and looked ahead to the new century, Blanche did an informal but frank assessment of her personal attributes and decided that she had sense enough not to be helpless. She knew that she could not spell and had handwriting "like hen tracks . . . disconnected, unformed and inadequate in material." (These insights from her college days may explain why she did not become the dedicated diary-keeper that Oakes was.) She admitted to indulging in daydreaming. Being trustful, honest, persistent and woefully critical were to her credit; a lack of bril-liance and an inability to entertain were on the debit side. Above all, she was very happy. She was told she was making good progress with her art work but wanted to do even better. "I feel somehow a power in me to do something that grows with added experience. And, oh joy, I have a fierce desire to work and work at it—I will succeed."[10]

Blanche first met her future husband when her brother Butler invited Oakes to dinner at the Ames's home in Lowell, Massachusetts in 1897. Butler also attended a Smith College dance and brought Oakes along. By the next year Oakes was sending her presents, including orchids, and just as she was turning twenty-one he sent her an expensive set of art books with her name embossed on the leather covers. Blanche saw it as an excep-tionally thoughtful gift though one outside the bounds of propriety since

8. Clark, *My Dear Mrs. Ames*, 51.

9. Crane, "Blanche Ames: Artist and Activist," 8.

10. Crane, "Blanche Ames: Artist and Activist," 7.

he was no more than her friend. However, Oakes was clearly smitten. He chose another highly unusual gift for Blanche once they were engaged. Where the gift of a microscope and slide kit would not have occurred to most young men and would not have appealed to most young women, Blanche and her fiancé were anything but typical. He gave her lessons on viewing the cross section of an orchid petal. That started them on their way to becoming a harmonious and devoted couple, each interested in what the other was interested in and sharing it, as their daughter Pauline later wrote in the Introduction to her father's *Jottings*.[11] First, however, they had to deal with the predictable and unsettling tensions that arose at the time of their engagement and marriage.

In her close examination of the influences that predisposed Blanche to become a public figure for reform, historian Anne Biller Clark found that marriage upset her subject's "sunny, generous, and optimistic" view of life and sense of "personal independence and autonomy." Furthermore, Blanche struggled to "preserve her personhood, her opinions, her vigor and her art, while contending with the constrictions of the traditional female sphere of her own marriage and motherhood."[12] She wanted to trust in Oakes's declarations about marriage as a *partnership*, yet "Oakes was but one of the liberal-minded men of his day who found that it is one thing to preach women's equality as an abstract principle and quite another to live it."[13]

Moreover, both Blanche and Oakes were uncomfortable in the company of their prospective in-laws, who were very different. Blanche's mother had strong convictions but seemed unconventional and free-spirited when compared to Oakes's mother, a Victorian matriarch who disapproved of independent-minded women, specifically the beautiful, high-spirited, athletic and artsy young woman who had captured her son's heart. In addition, Anna C. Ames, having been widowed, was jealous of the amount of time her son spent with his fiancée and her family in Lowell, which surely did not sit well with the bride-to-be and did not bode well for the young couple taking up residence, at Oakes's insistence, in the senior Mrs. Ames's home in North Easton after the wedding and for the next six years.

As for decisions about the wedding ceremony itself, Oakes made it his prerogative to take charge of the arrangements, altering plans made

11. Plimpton, P., Introduction, *Jottings of a Harvard Botanist*, 24.
12. Clark, *My Dear Mrs. Ames*, 59.
13. Clark, *My Dear Mrs. Ames*, 61.

by Blanche's parents for the music—Oakes wanted musicians from the Boston Symphony Orchestra—and for their choice of officiant—Unitarian clergy rather than Episcopal. Regarding religion, the Benjamin Butler family had had little time for it and the next generation was equally secular, save for Adelbert's interest in Unitarianism.[14] Adelbert's and Blanche's daughter Blanche (the fourth generation in the Ames Family line) could be nominally considered a Unitarian after her marriage to Oakes.[15] One assessment of her religious observance and intent to "do good" throughout her long life said "she sought social reform in this world and not consolation in the next."[16]

Oakes intended to break with tradition in another way. Believing that a wedding ring signified bondage, Oakes had decided to give a ring to his bride privately, not during the ceremony; but both of the mothers-in-law managed to overrule him on that. When Blanche, caught between loyalty to her betrothed and fealty to her parents, tried to remain neutral, Oakes made it clear that he expected her complete support. As far as it is known, there were not many other instances of Blanche giving in so easily throughout their long married life.[17] It turned out that Blanche ended up with *two* wedding rings and always wore both of them. When Blanche told her mother that Oakes would not give her a ring during the marriage ceremony because it represented bondage to him, her mother gave her the ring her grandmother Sarah Hildreth Butler had worn. The second one came from Oakes after his mother and sisters insisted he buy a ring for Blanche. Their daughter Pauline said that Blanche had a habit of touching the rings for courage when she faced difficult situations.[18]

The following are words Oakes used within a single paragraph in his diary to describe the years following his marriage to Blanche: *blessed time, serenity everywhere, rapid rebounds from depressions of the spirit* (caused by insufficient funds to cover household expenses), *pinnacle of optimism, tranquility.* Serenity, tranquility, indeed! Was Oakes really so oblivious to Blanche's discomfort in the years immediately following their marriage

---

14. Clark, *My Dear Mrs. Ames*, 32.

15. The Unitarian-Universalist Congregation of Frederick, Maryland named its art gallery after Blanche Ames, recognizing her as "an exceptional Unitarian Universalist who serves as an inspiration to us today."

16. Clark, *My Dear Mrs. Ames*, 55.

17. Clark, *My Dear Mrs. Ames*, 68-69.

18. Plimpton, P., Introduction, *Jottings of a Harvard Botanist*, 5.

when they resided in his parents' house in North Easton? He probably was. As he looked back on that time in *Jottings*, "I lived day to day delightfully absorbed in things I thought would go on forever!"[19]

Meanwhile, the ever-loving wife and mother of his children needed more room to spread her wings. Living with Oakes's mother in North Easton had quickly become unbearable for Blanche. Anna C. Ames, accustomed to gentility and refinement, disapproved of her free-spirited daughter-in-law and her zest for physical activity. Unconsciously or deliberately, Blanche would upset her mother-in-law, for example by walking barefoot and by racing horses with Oakes. The friction only increased when Blanche took the children to live with her family in Lowell because the children's nurse contracted pneumonia and she feared that there was danger of infection. Oakes saw this as another vote for her family over his.

The discord escalated into a marital feud when Oakes questioned Blanche's shortcomings and she accused him of paying more attention to his orchids than to his children. She needed him to understand how marriage had added to her burdens. If Oakes was free to choose research and teaching over a career in the lucrative family business, she insisted, why shouldn't she be able to pursue her art, hold strong opinions, and find a way to live as a modern woman in America? Was it possible for them to live as husband and wife in a way that recognized the equality of both?[20] With their beliefs and temperaments sorely tested, this set-to led to a shared acknowledgment that they needed their own place. Indeed, as we shall see, in the early years of their marriage Blanche and Oakes would struggle to separate themselves enough from their respective birth families in order to achieve their independence as a young family and as partners in science and in matters of social and political reform.[21]

Despite the insufficiency and inconstancy of his salary as an instructor and then as assistant professor of botany at Harvard, Oakes had the means to purchase tracts of land in North Easton and build what became the Borderland mansion, which will be described in the next chapter. They set about acquiring and renovating the old Tisdale place, a farmhouse some four miles from North Easton, where they would live temporarily until their permanent home could be built. An excerpt from Oakes's diary reveals how complete was their reconciliation: "Blanche and I are tasting

19. Ames, O., *Jottings of a Harvard Botanist*, 66.
20. Friend, "Borderland—The Life and Times of Blanche Ames Ames."
21. Clark, *My Dear Mrs. Ames*, 11.

lasting happiness to fullness now, and as we look forward to the completion of our little house and the development of our estate, our enthusiasm rises beyond control. To have a house of our very own to do with what we please, to have land on which to exercise the most inordinate of whims, is an experience to match which we know nothing in our past."[22]

Oakes's daily diary, which he kept from 1898 to his death in 1950, recorded details and impressions of his collecting trips, described the books he wrote and the journals to which he contributed, and recapped correspondence to family and colleagues. The diaries contained "autobiographical rambles and jottings" for his grandchildren and their descendants . . . "something of me that will be a part of them so long as they may live."[23] Clearly, he was a *chronicler*—his reports were as apt to describe his "interior" weather as the everyday kind—and Blanche was more of a *doer*. Oakes was a quiet, sensitive, reserved man (some would say reserved to the point of being aloof, diffident, and austere), who preferred to express his thoughts and feelings in diaries and letters while Blanche was a lively, outgoing woman known for delighting in controversy, according to their daughter Pauline.

Pauline described her parents' partnership this way. "It goes without saying that she worked with my father in everything he undertook, whether it was illustrating his books, being the architect for the house they were building, hearing his lectures, and advising and helping him in his University work."[24] With Oakes absorbed in his scholarly pursuits and administrative duties, it fell to Blanche to devise plans for the causeways and dams on the ponds and, later on, a water circulation system for the swimming pool. "They were a remarkable pair, complementing each other, not only in their capabilities but in their natures," Pauline observed. When Oakes was moody, Blanche counteracted with her gaiety. Oakes could be charming and interesting and or he could be silent, leaving Blanche to carry the conversation at mealtimes. Regardless, it was understood that "Mother always came first."[25] His scientific studies and work at the University came next, and then presumably his children.

22. Ames, O., *Jottings of a Harvard Botanist*, 243.
23. Ames, O., *Jottings of a Harvard Botanist*, 37.
24. Plimpton, P., Introduction, *Jottings of a Harvard Botanist*, 21.
25. Plimpton, P., Introduction, *Jottings of a Harvard Botanist*, 22–23.

# 3

# Creating Borderland

*"The realization of a beautiful dream"*
—OAKES AMES

B LANCHE AND OAKES LIVED at The Homestead in North Easton with Oakes's mother, Anna C. Ames, from 1900–1906 during which time their first two children, Pauline and Oliver, were born. As mentioned in chapter 2, conflict simmered between Blanche and her mother-in-law. Oakes was her baby, the youngest of her six children and a mama's boy who was tied to her apron strings (not that his mother ever really needed to wear an apron). Blanche struggled for autonomy in the marriage.[1] Traditionally, husbands were the decision makers and wives were "second-class citizens." Oakes claimed to believe that marriage was a contract or partnership between equals. Acting on that belief, however, would mean thwarting a heartfelt wish to keep his mother happy. As explained in chapter 2, he was quite comfortable with the arrangements at The Homestead and saw no need to upset them, until, that is, he finally recognized Blanche's distress and the damage it could do to his marriage. Anna C. Ames was particularly attached to him and was very angry with Oakes and Blanche for daring to move out to a place of their own. Fortunately, she and they later reconciled.

Here is how Oakes came around and Blanche got her way. His letters to Blanche from London in October and November 1905 revealed a slow awakening to the decisions he would have to make if the marriage was to survive. The correspondence spanned the three weeks Oakes spent studying collections and herbaria in London for the British Museum and the Kew collections at the Royal Botanic Gardens, accompanied by his two

---

1. Clark, *My Dear Mrs.* Ames.

North Easton assistants, Dr. Robert G. Leavitt, a plant morphologist, and Alva A. Eaton, a scientist and plant collector. While he was away, Blanche, Pauline, and Oliver stayed first with her mother in Lowell and then with her sister Sarah Ames Borden in Fall River. Aboard the *S.S. Saxonia* to England, Oakes passed the time taking walks on deck and doing some work with his microscope dissecting flowers and drawing on herbarium sheets in his stateroom.

Once comfortably ensconced in the Hotel Metropole in London, feeling homesick and lonely he began musing about his good fortune in meeting Blanche, the exhilaration he felt in her company, the companionship and communion they shared. Having chosen his way (that is, his life's work), he knew that she had "the power and opportunity to broaden it." Indeed, he went on, "Is it not our moral duty to standardize the other fellow's work and make life glorious where it is most keenly felt?"[2] This line of thought seemed to trigger an encouraging word to Blanche about the series of drawings she was doing for a new edition of *Gray's Manual of Botany*, and he wrote about his visit to the National Gallery to admire the paintings of Turner and others. A few weeks later, when he was preparing to return home, Oakes mentioned that Alva Eaton, who went to Paris in his stead, had been to the French engravers with Blanche's drawings. The engravers were wild about her drawings and could start engraving, no fixing up was necessary.

Far away from home, Oakes felt the need to express his love for Blanche: "I know that it is you, all the time, who order and rule my life and inclinations . . . I feel the need of your presence to make my life full and happy . . . . "[3] He had also reached an important turning point, conceding that his decision to live in his mother's house was not fair or kind to Blanche. He would make amends, make every sacrifice to ensure her happiness: "To be happy, really happy, we must hold strongly to the belief in equality, and cultivate intensively that mutual ground . . . . "[4] He had never known anyone whose nature was as good and noble as hers, so he would do what was best and wisest and give her a home of comfort and freedom which would be for the good of both of them . . . and for the proper development of the little ones whose lives and futures were largely in their care. Therefore, he was ready to make the move and undertake any expenditure to "purchase a condition" acceptable to her. They would have a home of

2. Ames, O., *Jottings of a Harvard Botanist*, 189.
3. Ames, O., *Jottings of a Harvard Botanist*, 192.
4. Ames, O., *Jottings of a Harvard Botanist*, 194.

their own as she had been urging (and he would have all the bookcases he needed). This had to be music to Blanche's ears!

Not so fast. As soon as he received a letter from Blanche in which she proposed acquiring the property adjacent to her parents' summer home at Bay View near Gloucester on Cape Ann in Massachusetts, Oakes begged her not to send him "her practical plans which annoy . . . and send a chill across the ocean."[5] The very thought of losing his natal home in North Easton upset him terribly. They should wait to form their own plans once he was returned from his trip and could confer face to face, not listening to "too many outside influences" (he meant her family members' opinions about having a permanent residence of one's own). Meanwhile, if she could sympathize with his current "atmosphere," she would stick to more soothing topics in her letters. Oakes again heard from Blanche five days later, their letters having crossed in the mail, and was dismayed to read that her enthusiasm for the Bay View purchase was at high pitch. He repeated that he could not share her feelings about Bay View. Nevertheless, he understood her desire for a place where she could feel at home and happy, so he would stir heaven and earth to provide it because her happiness was of paramount importance to him.[6]

We can dip into a chapter of Harriet Stevens Robey's family saga *Bay View* for insight into Oakes's reluctance to live among Blanche's kin, a entire chapter in *Bay View* called, for good reason, "The In-Laws." This generally perceptive niece of Oakes and Blanche (Harriet's mother was Blanche's sister Edith Ames Stevens) knew that Oakes was willing to join in family vacations of limited duration at Bay View, but the family's clannishness and insider camaraderie put such a strain on the in-laws that "the in-laws felt like out-laws."[7] Uncle Oakes Ames, world-famous for his botanical work, did something extraordinary about it, Robey recalled. At a family gathering in the early 1900s that included Grandmother and Grandfather Ames (a.k.a General and Mrs. Adelbert Ames) and all their daughters and husbands, Oakes pinned an emblem on the lapel of each son-in-law. The emblem had a lemon fastened to a ribbon and a tag indicating membership in the "In-Law Club." Oakes, betraying a "stern smile

5. Ames, O., *Jottings of a Harvard Botanist*, 209.
6. Ames, O., *Jottings of a Harvard Botanist*, 215–216.
7. Robey, *Bay View*, 331.

which, for that very reserved man, was a laugh," then led them in singing "A Lemon in the Garden of Love."[8]

Among the four sons-in-law, Oakes stood out for his height, austerity, and for being what Robey deemed the only true intellectual in the family. All four of the men had gone to Harvard, yet they were quite different. Harriet Robey remembered Oakes this way: "He was accustomed to giving commands and being obeyed. He was a lover of nature, beauty, and books. He too, like my father, was quite asocial, at least in his later years."[9] Although otherwise a keen observer, having been a psychiatric social worker for forty years, Harriet Robey misjudged at least one thing about her Uncle Oakes—in those early years of marriage, he had *not* accepted his wife's close ties to her birth family, particularly to her mother.

As was typical of his letters to Blanche, Oakes would abruptly switch from pouring out his personal concerns to less contentious topics, such as her choice of a Pierce Arrow automobile, which he strongly endorsed, and his decision about documentation of the Philippine orchids at Kew. At another point he wondered whether Blanche could make sense out of the wretched construction and hurried sentences of his letters, trusting to her familiarity with his mannerisms and odd expressions to know what he really intended.

While living with Anna C. Ames at The Homestead in North Easton and even before contemplating construction of their own house, the young couple had been quietly buying up land using intermediaries who were not named Ames, lest publicity drive up the price. They were farming some of the land and leaving the rest as a wildlife preserve. Oakes's diary entries about Borderland, commencing in 1906, describe the tracts of North Easton wooded land and bodies of water Oakes and Blanche managed to acquire for their estate and their attempts to keep the negotiations quiet. Nevertheless, word got around and a reporter for the *Brockton Times* came close to the truth, speculating that Mr. Ames might be planning a hunting and game preserve, or—on account of the unsurpassed beauty of the view from the highest point of land between Boston and Newport—a country estate similar to the famous Frederick Lothrop Ames

8. "A Lemon in the Garden of Love" was a humorous song recorded in 1906 by Billy Murray that asks why, if only peaches grow in the garden of love, he picked a bitter lemon. In today's parlance, many would say it smacks of misogyny.

9. Robey, *Bay View*, 333.

Estate.[10] (Oakes's cousin Frederick Lothrop Ames, who lived from 1835 to 1893, was an heir to the Ames Shovel Works, a director of forty railroads, including the Old Colony and the Union Pacific, a real estate investor, and, of particular interest to his nephew, he was also an avid amateur orchid gardener. His former estate became the campus of Stonehill College in 1948.) With the assistance of a local surveyor, Oakes and Blanche began systematically visiting, evaluating, and purchasing contiguous properties, always orienting themselves in relation to the pond called Wilbur's (now Leach Pond) above which their new house would stand. The mounting expenses were worrisome, he wrote, but the couple was very happy with their outdoor life and the prospect of a new home.

Oakes's observations in a lengthy paragraph written February 25, 1906 are significant in establishing the couple's *modus operandi* for the immediate future and the decades to come: they would have the courage and take the time and initiative to figure out how to solve problems themselves, whether hydraulic, mechanical, or architectural, and learn much from the experience. "Necessity is a marvelous tutor for the inexperienced and usually develops faculties of which we have had no previous care," he noted.[11] Indolent members of the upper class, in his opinion, fail to acquire practical knowledge by hiring other people to solve their problems; this stimulates enterprise among those less wealthy but debilitates society.

Oakes did not spend every day on serious endeavors; he was not above occasionally succumbing to "luxurious idleness, day dreams and air castles." As he confided to his journal in March 1906, "I am living a romantic existence just now, and I feel that the longings of many years are being fulfilled." His meadowlands and forests are "the realization of a beautiful dream."[12] Euphoria persisted in the April 7, 1906 diary entry. After he and Blanche took an invigorating walk and visited the brook, the spring, and one of the ponds, all near to bursting their banks after three days of rain, he enthused about conjugal bliss and the renovations at the Tisdale farmhouse, built in 1810 on Mountain Street in Sharon, where they would live temporarily.

Oakes was back down to earth at the end of the next month. He returned in a melancholy frame of mind from a visit with his mother, who had been in a bad mood and berated him again for deciding to move out of her house. He could overlook her "unreason and unkindness," but was

---

10. Ames, O., *Jottings of a Harvard Botanist*, 225.

11. Ames, O., *Jottings of a Harvard Botanist*, 237.

12. Ames, O., *Jottings of a Harvard Botanist*, 239.

saddened by it. Her criticisms hit the intended mark and had the effect of making him doubt, if only briefly, the wisdom of his actions. "As to my determination to cut adrift from the influences and atmosphere of the old home, time alone will show whether or not I have been guilty of a gross error."[13] We do not know whether Oakes confided in Blanche about these momentary qualms. A safe bet is that he knew better than to get her riled up over feelings that would quickly pass once he was busy hanging pictures in their new home, arranging books in his library, or taking a walk with her and the children.

Strained relations persisted. His mother tried retaliatory measures, forbidding Bolton, the supervisor of Oakes's botanical collection housed at The Homestead, access to her property and forbidding him to touch the orchids. Oakes had his men remove the orchids from her greenhouses and transport them to the Tisdale farmhouse where he and the family would be living until Borderland and a new herbarium could be built. His mother then sent word that she no longer wanted any milk from the cows at Oakes's farm; in fact she wanted the milk cows returned to her barn. After this was accomplished, Mrs. Ames changed her mind and the cows were sent back to Oakes's pasture. An exchange of letters followed in which pleas for understanding and kinder feelings won the day.

In May of 1906 when Blanche and Oakes were finally moving from his mother's house to the renovated Tisdale farmhouse, Oakes felt the need to state that he intended the diaries as a record of "a part of the life Blanche and I have lived together that will teach our children to know us as we were at a critical period of our lives and of theirs. If these children of ours are disposed to read such a formidable book as a parent's diary, they will surely learn from this one a great deal that should enlighten them in the ways of life and array before them the changes that make life spicy and sweet, flat and bitter. From it they will learn what little events will change the whole course of a man's existence and on what trivial matters depend the sadness or happiness of an ordinary human being."[14] And still later, he acknowledged that 1906 had been full of "unlooked-for results," a year during which Borderland had come to represent "a revolution of feelings, ideas, and thoughts."[15]

13. Ames, O., *Jottings of a Harvard Botanist*, 249.

14. Ames, O., *Jottings of a Harvard Botanist*, 245.

15. Ames, O., *Jottings of a Harvard Botanist*, 266.

The activity for the day of June 15 was the birth of their third child, an eight-pound boy, later to be named Amyas. In typical Oakes fashion, he noted in his diary the time that Blanche went upstairs with the doctor (3:15 a.m.), the time the "newcomer" arrived (an hour and fifteen minutes later), and the time he and the doctor sat down to breakfast (5:15 a.m.). It was beautiful, peaceful morning. Oakes "felt keenly" the want of sleep and took a nap on the sofa. About Blanche? He said that she and the "new acquisition" were well and that her mother had arrived. His very next entries concerned the rain, his geraniums, the rose garden and the strawberries.

Oakes wrote an appreciation of Blanche's mother after she visited them at The Homestead when Amyas was born: "She has a broad healthy view of life, regards petty affairs with extreme indifference and exhibits those delightful traits which develop strongly in people of firm purpose and strong character."[16] Blanche's mother could be controlling but she was not like Oakes's own mother, Anna C. Ames, who was later described by her granddaughter Pauline as "an imperious lady."[17] Pauline offset the criticism with appreciation for her grandmother's generosity to the townspeople of North Easton—building a gymnasium, donating band instruments for the high school—and for making her home and her automobile available to woman suffragists, lending financial support to the cause, and somehow managing to recruit Father Daniel Doran of Easton's Church of the Immaculate Conception to the suffragist ranks.

On a beautiful July day, just one month after Amyas's birth, Blanche and Oakes paddled their canoe on Wilbur's Pond and spent the afternoon raking sphagnum moss, dead leaves, twigs and branches from the pond bottom. They were thoroughly enjoying their new home, both deriving great pleasure from a sense of seclusion and ownership. Again in August, on a hot day when the air was heavy the two of them were clearing away shrubbery in preparation for a new pond to be called Pud's. Oakes merely said that the strenuous exercise made them feel "fairly well." Of course, if Blanche had wanted to avoid all this manual labor so soon after giving birth, she could easily have made excuses. For that matter, there was no need for Oakes to get hot and sweaty doing jobs his workmen could do. The following words from Blanche as recorded in Oakes's diary are telling: "Isn't it strange that we two should have come out here to live? What a wonderful thing human affection is! Neither of us alone would have

16. Ames, O., *Jottings of a Harvard Botanist*, 8.
17. Ames, O., *Jottings of a Harvard Botanist*, 8.

thought of doing what we have done together." To which Oakes appended this observation: "The fact is people, ordinary people, need mutual support in all extraordinary undertakings."[18] Evidently, they both relished working and playing together—studying new species and drawing orchids, making improvements to the Borderland property, in addition to walking, biking, canoeing, fishing, shooting ducks, and (far more terrifying, to Oakes) raising a family together.

The tracts of land Oakes acquired amounted to some 1,200 acres of farmland, woods, fields, meadows, wetlands, and ponds located four miles from the town center, away from the busy Ames Shovel Works and from the houses of Oakes's relatives. The countryside offered exercise and fresh air and long walks or horseback rides into town. They could help workers to clear brush, cut trees, drain a swamp and dam it up to create a pond for swimming in summer and ice skating in winter. They planned to cut ice blocks from the ponds and store them with sawdust between the layers in an icehouse for later use in pantry and kitchen "iceboxes." (In time, this would be the setting for grandson Edward (Ned) Ames's icehouse adventure, recounted in the next chapter.) Vegetables would be stored in the root cellar and corn stored in its crib. Dairy cows in the barn would provide milk, cream, butter, and ice cream. They would have workhorses and riding horses that could be used to pull carriages, and they would raise chickens and turkeys. Blanche later designed cages with wire floors that kept turkeys off the floor, thus preventing black-head disease, and she wrote articles describing her disease-prevention efforts.

Borderland changed everything for Blanche. Having her own home "allowed her to live more like the new woman she longed to be."[19] They could live and play close to nature. She could have an art studio and workshop on the third floor. Their home would be a gathering place for like-minded men and women. "It was a stable, old-fashioned family life," daughter Pauline said, filled with music lessons, reading, berry picking, exploring, hide-and-seek in the hay barns, horseback riding, and tennis.[20] Her parents won mixed doubles tennis tournaments all along the North Shore. Her father, ordinarily "very severe and reserved" with the children, was "an interested and endlessly patient coach" when it came to athletics. Pauline's younger sister Evelyn—Evelyn had arrived in 1910, four years

18. Ames, O., *Jottings of a Harvard Botanist*, 262.

19. Friend, "Borderland—The Life and Times of Blanche Ames Ames."

20. Plimpton, P., *Jottings of a Harvard Botanist*, 14.

after Amyas—benefitted from Oakes's tennis lessons. Oakes would drop a handkerchief on his side of the court and challenge her to hit it. When she was in her mid-sixties Evelyn became serious about tennis again, played top-level doubles, and won the National Singles Clay Court Championship in her age category. Social life at Borderland and in Boston revolved around family, Oakes's colleagues, and college friends.

As respite from the hours Oakes spent researching and writing about orchids, he might take a long walk with Blanche after tea or feed the rabbits with one of the children, or go skating, play hockey, go motoring, play tennis on their own court or golf at nearby Thorny Lea in Brockton. Nurse Linda Williams, who attended Blanche in her last years, heard stories from Blanche about the fun she and Oakes had had together in the early 1900s, doing messy outdoor chores—cutting firewood, farming, gardening, raising chickens and turkeys—and getting a vigorous workout. A copy of a Borderland Turkey Farm ad can be found on page 385 of *Jottings*. The flyer warns buyers to make sure they are getting genuine home-grown birds—the market being flooded with thousands of inferior-grade turkeys at Thanksgiving and Christmas that were raised in western states, shipped to Vermont, then reshipped to Massachusetts and sold as Vermont turkeys.

"Native Milk-fed Turkeys from Borderland Turkey Farm

Oakes Ames, Proprietor

For Thanksgiving, Christmas, Week-end Parties

Write to: Superintendent, Borderland Farm, North Easton, Massachusetts

Telephone North Easton 77–4

Order direct from the farm and know that you are getting tender, young, native turkeys. Carefully prepared and delivered to your door, or iced and sent by parcel post or express, or you may wish to motor out to the farm and choose your own bird."

Nurse Linda Williams also heard from Blanche how the four children were kept busy with tasks like tending the fireplace in each room. Apparently, the Ames children were not coddled like the children in most wealthy families.

In addition to his scholarly pursuits, Oakes was very fond of reading the classics. On January 24, 1907 he selected *Antony and Cleopatra* "to change the trend of [his] thoughts" after "concentrated application" (that is, strenuous mental effort) on the Philippine orchid genera and on the final revision of the manuscript for Fascicle II of *Orchidaceae*. In the same diary entry is a long soliloquy on country life compared with the stimulation of city life, the former being much healthier, and on the importance of having deep-seated interests to forestall ennui and discontent. He continued to be troubled by existential questions, remarking that he was thirty-three and, without a religious sense, still pondering his "strange views of life."[21]

In February of 1907, Oakes announced with great excitement in his diary that he and Blanche were planning a new, English-style country house. It would be more substantial than the perfectly adequate Tisdale farmhouse in which they were then living, and it would be a house of fireproof construction whose main feature would be a library. By 1908 they had hired an architect, Joseph M. A. Darrach, to design the house, and by 1909 the architect's plans for an expensive, pretentious structure had been summarily rejected. Quite miffed, Mr. Darrach sued. Blanche experienced one of the headaches to which she was prone, then decided that she would draw up her own plans for the house with the help of an engineering firm. This was but one example of the couple's shared resolve to take the time and initiative to figure out how to solve problems themselves, whether hydraulic, mechanical, or architectural, and learn much from the experience, necessity being a marvelous tutor for the inexperienced—those lessons Oakes emphasized in his diary and clearly wanted his children to learn.

Dissatisfied with the architect's grandiose plans for the house, Blanche took over the design and construction management for the mansion and hired the Concrete Engineering Company to draw plans according to her specifications. She calculated the engineering measurements for the causeways and dams built on the ponds surrounding the mansion as well.[22] In the end, Borderland had everything she and Oakes wanted, including electricity, central heating, and the very first automobile garage in Easton. The garage was underneath the servants' quarters in the east wing of the mansion. As many as eight men were employed to do outdoor work on the Borderland property and there were eight house servants. The library was in the west wing. A barn was located about one hundred yards from the east wing of the mansion. (It burned down in the 1970s and a corncrib is the last reminder of its presence.)

21. Ames, O., *Jottings of a Harvard Botanist*, 271.

22. Ames Mansion, part of the Borderland Historic District, National Register of Historic Places. See National Park Service.

The Darrach suit dragged on through 1911 and into 1912, adding to the expense of house and road building and making for Oakes "a hell of a year." But he cheered up when the library was finally finished and he, with assistance from the children, could arrange his books and journals on the shelves—the *Journal of the Linnean Society* and the *Journal of Botany* were the first to be placed. They also planted the Ampelapsis vines (ornamental climbing plants also called porcelain berry, peppervine, and wild grape) that cover the outside walls of the house to this day.

In addition to the need for a completely fireproof residence where their precious books (eventually numbering 10,000) and paintings would be safe, Blanche and Oakes had several other reasons for building Borderland. They wanted to get away from town and its manufacturing operations and be close to nature, as previously mentioned. They aimed to spend no more than fifty thousand dollars. Evidently, Oakes's salary as a junior member of the faculty at Harvard was small, but the family fortune from the Ames Shovel Works was enormous and Oakes had the means to purchase tracts of land in North Easton and to undertake construction of the Borderland mansion. And they had agreed to build at a distance from Oakes's mother Anna C. Ames and their many other Ames relatives. It would be a stone-clad, all concrete, European-style house with interesting angles and with windows everywhere for views of the grounds and windows that worked like doors for easy access to the outdoors, to sun porches, and to the rooftop.

It is interesting to pause and consider why Blanche and Oakes chose the name "Borderland" for their estate, as it can be interpreted in several quite disparate ways—the property's location between the towns of Sharon and North Easton in Massachusetts being the most obvious. The name could also signify the physical boundary between the hunting and fishing territories of the Massachusetts and Wampanoag Indian tribes. Blanche and possibly Oakes might have thought of it as delineating the distance from the properties of his Ames relatives. Extending this interpretation, historian Anne Biller Clark has posited that their removal to a place of their own on their own land, away from both Oakes's and Blanche's family homes, entailed a decision "to live their lives on the borderland of acceptable behavior for their class . . . confident in their right to make their own choices, supportive of each other, and willing to act outside and beyond the socially accepted boundaries of the elite."[23] Moreover, the metaphor signified lives

23. Clark, *My Dear Mrs. Ames*, 74–75.

"on the border of new realms to be conquered, a sort of Borderland of the soul that kept Blanche alive and active into extreme old age."[24]

A different yet related interpretation by Anne Digby would take us from class to gender norms by attributing the meaning of *borderland* to the Victorian ideological divide between the public or masculine sphere and the private or feminine sphere; that is, "an intermediate or semi-detached area between public and private," which "alerts us to the presence of a boundary, frontier or brink in gender relations."[25] Although, as stated previously, Oakes claimed early on to believe that marriage was a partnership between equals, his innate preference for privacy and Blanche's greater confidence when in public served to reverse the expected pattern and sometimes made it a challenge to live up to the partnership ideal. Of all the possible interpretations of the name, Digby's is probably not one that the couple themselves would have publicly acknowledged.

Blanche and Oakes Ames's 22,212 square foot mansion was completed in 1912 with multiple rooms, bathrooms, and fireplaces. Built of fieldstone gathered from local stone walls, it had floors of cement and was entirely fireproof. The interior of the house today remains largely the same as it was more than a century ago, Visitor Service Supervisor Paul Clifford assured me during a tour. The estate changed hands in 1971 when Blanche had passed away and the family made sure that it would become a state park managed by the Massachusetts Department of Conservation and Recreation (MDCR). Clifford assists Borderland's Park Supervisor with responsibilities ranging from land management to archiving precious relics and overseeing special events. A history enthusiast and nature lover, he is painstakingly transcribing Oakes's diaries, the voluminous daily record kept by Oakes for fifty-two years. And, in another departure from his usual routines, Clifford is credited with going "above and beyond when it comes to not only preserving the tangibles in and around the palatial mansion but also keeping the treasured stories connected to Blanche and her husband, Oakes Ames, alive."[26] The year 2022 was especially busy when Borderland was celebrating the fiftieth anniversary of both its opening as a state park, delayed one year by the COVID pandemic, as well as the incorporation of the Friends of

24. Clark, *My Dear Mrs. Ames*, 1.

25. Digby, "Victorian Values and Women in Public and Private," 195–215.

26. Friend, "Borderland—The Life and Times of Blanche Ames Ames."

Borderland,[27] bringing together local vendors, businesses, non-profits, community members, and friends from near and far.

In the dining room at Borderland, a large antique chandelier in the shape of a ship is suspended from the middle of the ceiling over a table sized for family of six. Our knowledgeable tour guide assumes that Oakes sat at one end of the dining table and Blanche at the other as was the conventional arrangement. (In the next chapter, the grandchildren's stories have the grandparents seated "amid ships," as it were.) The cream-colored acoustic ceiling tiles that were installed in the 1950s have a distinctive oak leaf pattern, a motif that Oakes would have enjoyed. Blanche could step on a button beneath the carpet to summon the butler to bring in food from the adjacent pantry. The dining room, like rooms throughout the house, has a wall of windows, some of which actually do work like doors for easy access to the outdoors and nature. Likely due to Oakes's extremely shy nature, the couple did not socialize and entertain much; their guests were usually family members.

The living room, called the Music Room today, has heavy drapes that were left behind by the filmmakers when the 1984 comedy "Ghostbusters," or possibly the 2019 thriller "Knives Out," was filmed at Borderland. American impressionist Edmund Charles Tarbell's oil painting of Blanche has a commanding presence in this room. In 1907 she sat for Tarbell's portrait, commissioned by her husband. No doubt to please Oakes, Blanche is in her wedding gown, bedecked with pink ribbons, and she carries a bouquet of pink flowers. There were at least twenty-four sittings that took place at The Homestead. What helped Blanche to pass the time while holding the pose was discussing oil painting methods with Mr. Tarbell (1862–1938). In the process, Blanche was influenced by the techniques of the Boston School, led by Tarbell, who was director of the School of the Museum of Fine Arts at the time. Oakes enjoyed watching him at work and on January 18 jotted down this Tarbell tip in his diary, perhaps as a favor to his wife: to obtain the proper relations between the color masses, apply color to the edges of a drawing and work from there to the center. When the finished portrait of Blanche was exhibited in Boston and Philadelphia, the reviews were positive and the couple was "reassured by its critical acceptance."[28]

27. The Friends of Borderland is a 501(c)(3) nonprofit volunteer organization that assists the Massachusetts Department of Conservation and Recreation in preserving and interpreting the natural, historical, and cultural resources of Borderland State Park in North Easton and Sharon.

28. Crane, "Blanche Ames: Artist and Activist," 22.

According to a Brockton Art Museum retrospective, portraiture was Blanche's preferred field. Blanche considered traditional oil portraiture to be "the best in art which incorporates the tried and true principles of artistic expression through the centuries" by remaining faithful to an accurate and sensitive (or *genteel*, as Tarbell would have it) representation of one's subject.[29] She had seen exhibitions of the newer painting styles of modernists in European museums while on her honeymoon and during later trips abroad, but she preferred the "tried and true" over the radical.

On top of all her other projects and responsibilities, somehow Blanche carved out time for portraiture. Before long, recognizing her talent, family members and other notables began commissioning oil portraits from Blanche. Some can be seen at Borderland, others hang at Dartmouth College, Phillips Exeter Academy, Barnard College, the Mississippi Hall of Governors—her father in his Union Army uniform—and the Massachusetts Horticultural Society. One of several paintings of Oakes hangs prominently in the Music Room at Borderland. In this room too are oil paintings of Blanche's mother and father, Blanche Butler Ames and General Adelbert Ames, and Oakes's mother, Anna C. Ames. And a prominently placed photo of Blanche and her Smith College basketball team recalls one of the formative yet unconventional experiences in her long life. (When I played college basketball in the early 1960s, which predated Title IX of the Education Amendments of 1972, it was still unconventional.)

In his *Jottings*, a June 1931 letter from Oakes to his daughter Pauline mentioned her mother keeping busy on and off with her painting and drawing. He thought her botanical drawings were quite good. In fact, her reputation was growing and her published drawings were well received. As to portraiture, when she was finished working on an oil painting of cousin Winthrop's father, Oakes reported, Blanche would start on a portrait of an ancestor of Sohier Welch. The name Sohier Welch caught my attention because he was married to Margaret Pearmain Welch, the Boston socialite and activist who co-founded and led the Birth Control League of Massachusetts with Blanche Ames Ames. (See chapter 6.) Margaret Welch also has special significance because she is the subject of my 2017 biography, and it was the research for that book that first piqued my curiosity about Blanche Ames Ames.[30] Small world, indeed!

---

29. Crane, "Blanche Ames: Artist and Activist," 10–11.

30. Fideler, *Margaret Pearmain Welch (1893-1984)*.

The library at Borderland takes one's breath away because of its impressive size and beauty. Two stories tall, it occupies the entire west wing of the mansion. One door on the second floor connects directly to the mansion's grand staircase and another door connects to the master bedroom and also to stairs leading to Oakes's laboratory, which was downstairs below the library and contained steel cases housing dried orchid specimens, microscopes, and scientific instruments. A balcony on all four sides of the library's second floor is made of thick glass that allows light to pass through. Hanging over the balcony railings and beside them are treasures collected on the couple's trips abroad, such as Indonesian shadow puppets, a large bronze dragon from China, small Turkish tapestries, and a golden ceremonial sword given to Blanche's grandfather General Benjamin F. Butler from the people of Lowell, Massachusetts. For many years, the bronze dragon had guarded Borderland's swimming pool. It was removed to the library when the estate became a state park in 1971 because its ruby eyes were already missing and the Massachusetts Department of Conservation and Recreation wanted to prevent further vandalism.

One's eyes are drawn to the full bookshelves reaching from floor to ceiling all around the library. Oakes's book collection meant everything to him: "But I like to consider the book the crystalized product of a human brain. I remove from my mind all thought of head and body and clothes and just look upon a book as a brain or part of a brain, bound for its value and kept on a library shelf to teach the generation that is and the generation to be, what is best in life, and I extend this idea, and look on my library as an equal brain; there are some corners of it not always active, in other words here are the rarely used brain cells."[31]

Visitor Service Supervisor Paul Clifford explained how Blanche thought it fitting to donate about half of Oakes's valuable collection to the University of Texas after her husband passed away because the university was creating a botanical library and the director was a colleague of Oakes. She took the trouble to stamp each book with Oakes's name, but it was later discovered that the University of Texas colleague stamped his own name on top of Oakes's. Later, the Massachusetts Department of Conservation and Recreation filled the empty bookshelves with volumes from the basement, Congressional annals, and the like.

Another perspective on this story comes from grandson Edward (Ned) Ames who remembers his grandmother objecting to Harvard's taking a work

31. Ames, O., *Jottings of a Harvard Botanist*, 106–107.

table used by students at the Arnold Arboretum for its use in Cambridge and, related to that protest, her decision to divert the planned gift of an early edition of Linnaeus that was a feature of the Borderland library from Harvard to the University of Texas. This occurred in the early 1950s when Oakes was gone and Blanche was challenging Harvard's more egregious actions in the Arnold Arboretum Controversy. (See chapter 8.)

Blanche's art reference books are on the shelves of the Borderland library's first floor. There is a cabinet containing Oakes's diaries, many small ones and larger ones, in which the professor meticulously recorded details and thoughts about his life. Blanche used to keep the diaries in an iron chest at Borderland. Her daughter Pauline surmised that its resemblance to a pirate's chest in the imaginations of the children was helped by a painting Blanche had made of the chest featuring a skull and pieces of eight and the macheté Oakes brought home from one of his trips to Cuba.[32] The 1924 oil painting called *Pirate Chest* was described in the Brockton Art Museum's 1982 catalogue as "a most unusual example of Blanche's oeuvre. A bold, colorful composition of startling objects." The curator of the exhibit "Blanche Ames: Artist and Activist" thought it might be a mood painting or an illustration for a story.[33]

The library's distinctive diamond-paned windows on two sides of the room were designed by Blanche so that sun streaming through yellow and green stained glass would light the room in a golden glow. There is a large, handsome table in the middle of the room and smaller tables and chairs are placed here and there. Kevin Friend's documentary about Borderland includes footage of Blanche dancing gleefully around the central library table in 1918 after hearing that the anti-suffrage Republican senator John Weeks was defeated by the pro-suffrage Democratic challenger David Walsh, whom she had backed even though she was a life-long Republican. (See chapter 5.) Two eight-foot tall candelabra stand at the far end of the room. Covering the concrete floor is a sumptuous wool rug in soft forest green with a figured border of gold, crimson, and green. Made by order in India to Oakes's specifications, the rug measures approximately twenty feet by thirty feet and weighs over one thousand pounds. When it arrived in 1915, Oakes declared the room was "now complete."

The second floor contains the master bedroom, whose doors open up to a sun porch, and bedrooms for the two daughters, Pauline and Evelyn.

32. Plimpton, P., *Jottings of a Harvard Botanist*, 221.
33. Crane, "Blanche Ames: Artist and Activist," 29.

Paintings in Pauline's room are of two of her children—young Sarah Plimpton and young Oakes Ames Plimpton—and Blanche's 1913 painting of an elm tree that is on the cover of the 1982 Brockton Art Museum catalogue. Blanche's drawings of orchids (the originals are at Harvard) and the charts she developed for Oakes's economic botany courses can be seen in the Orchid Room. Also on the second floor over the east wing of the house are the staff quarters—eight rooms for women, two rooms for men. There are skylights in the halls and a "call box" that is not as large as the one at Downton Abbey, but it served the same purpose.

The rooms of Blanche's and Oakes's two sons are on third floor. Information in Oliver's bedroom explains that Oliver was married to Ellen Moseley of the family for which Maudslay State Park on the Merrimack River in Newburyport is named, allowing the Visitor Service Supervisor to clarify that there are *two* state parks in the family. (Moseley is a variant of Maudesley or Maudesleigh, an old English name.) Amyas's bedroom is now called the Holbein Room due to the works displayed there, as Blanche was fascinated with Holbein's art. (In a 1916 letter to his wife who was summering at Bay View with the children while he was at home in North Easton, Oakes told Blanche he had on approval a series of eighty exquisitely engraved plates of Holbein's Portraits of the Court of Henry VIII that she might want to acquire for her library so she could study Holbein's use of color for flesh tones and garments. And, in February–May 2022, Sir Thomas More and other magnificent Holbein portraits were on display at the Morgan Library and Museum in Manhattan. "Holbein: Capturing Character" was the first major exhibition dedicated to the artist in the United States. Blanche would have rushed to see it!)

Nearby in Blanche's third-floor art studio is a recipe book for mixing colors and a bureau whose drawers are filled with thousands of small tubes of oil paints. On her easel sit the sketches and color codes for portraits she was working on in her eighties. Blanche's endearing portrait of her granddaughter Olivia at ten years of age hangs in the art studio. Blanche put water in the background of the painting because she knew her granddaughter, a Pisces, loved water and loved to swim. Olivia returned the portrait to Borderland in 2021 because, she explained, "It was simply time for the portrait to go back." A separate workroom features the color chart system Blanche developed with her brother Adelbert. (See chapter 1.) Tools lie on the workbench and shelves on an opposite wall hold specimens from Oakes's laboratory that were moved to her workroom.

What was a guest room is now the Military History Room, dedicated mainly to the exploits of Blanche's grandfather General Benjamin F. Butler. In addition to his desk and cot and many Civil War-era photos, there are framed letters of commendation: one thanking Captain John Butler (Blanche's great-grandfather) for his service in the War of 1812, signed by President James Madison; another thanking General Benjamin F. Butler for his service in the Civil War, signed by President Abraham Lincoln; and a third thanking General Adelbert Ames (Blanche's father) for service in the Spanish-American War, signed by President William McKinley.

A third-floor hallway is filled with photos of individual family houses, transcontinental railroad photos, and a montage depicting eleven mansions in Easton owned by Ames Shovel Company relatives that bears the title "Ames Family Country Estates, North Easton, Massachusetts." Other photos show local public buildings named after Ames relatives, such as Oliver Ames High School and Oakes Ames Memorial Hall. Sitting in this hallway is the 1899 self-portrait in plaster made by Blanche in her senior year at Smith College. (And after the new Easton elementary school named for Blanche Ames Ames opens in 2023, another photo can be added to the wall—see Epilogue.)

Visitor Service Supervisor Paul Clifford next showed a visitor Blanche's sewing room where an extra-large spool of thick thread still sits atop the sewing machine table. Apparently, the spool of thread gave her an idea during World War II for an invention: bringing down enemy airplanes during bombing raids by jamming their propellers with long, hanging threads suspended from barrage balloons and causing their engines to stall. The fiber she designed was lighter than the steel cables that were then used, allowing the balloons to rise higher and be more effective. She borrowed a light airplane from her son Oliver, who was a naval aviator, and experimented on the driving range, which was on the front lawn at Borderland. Experts were invited to a demonstration at Borderland, including Pentagon officials and Vannevar Bush, an inventor himself who had been dean of the school of engineering at MIT before becoming head of President Roosevelt's newly created Office of Scientific Research and Development in 1942. Following the successful demonstration, they did approve of her invention, but it came too late to be put into use before the war ended.

Stepping outside the house, a visitor sees a large bell mounted atop the roof. Its provenance is disturbing, for this was an old slave bell brought by Oakes from the Atkins Sugar Plantation in Soledad, Cuba, which lies near the southern coast of the island. In 1903 his mentor Dr. Goodale had sent Oakes to the Harvard Experiment Station on the plantation to escort a Dr. Willis, director of the Peridenia Gardens in Ceylon, to the Station and to evaluate the gardens and the sugar cane experiments in pollination and hybridization. Oakes had a sneaking suspicion that Dr. Willis—an administrator but not a researcher—knew little or nothing about sugar cane, and he was proved right. In a series of letters to Blanche from Cuba, Oakes spoke of his relief when his well-founded ideas for improving the Atkins gardens and for promoting sugar cane pollination were gratefully accepted. Oakes went on to speculate about what he could accomplish if only he had more time there. This wishful thinking became reality twenty-four years later when President Lowell put him in charge of the Atkins Gardens and Research Laboratory at Soledad as well as all the rest of Harvard's botanical institutions. (See chapter 8.)

In another letter Oakes commented on the ringing of the plantation's huge bell, formerly used to drive men to and from their work, "aided by the stinging lash," and he briefly expounded upon the atrocities of holding men in bondage. He later purchased the bell—one can only surmise the reason—and had it shipped to Borderland in 1910 where it was installed on the corner of the library roof. Once connected electrically to a clock in the library, it rang out the hours and could summon home children or grandchildren playing far afield. When the Massachusetts suffrage amendment failed on November 2, 1915, Blanche vowed to ring the bell every day until enfranchisement was achieved and she could celebrate. (See chapter 5.)

On the left side of the house when facing the front is a rock garden, reached by stone steps that wind down and around, leading to an arbor and on to what used to be the spring-fed swimming pool. Blanche transformed what had once been a bog garden into a swimming pool in the summer of 1930. In a letter to his daughter Pauline, Oakes described how her mother had put a crow bar into the bog to test its depth and found that it did not touch bottom. Discovering good springs nearby gave her a new idea. She hired a big digger to excavate mountains of earth from the hole, which was no longer a mere four feet across. And, with concrete work, granite blocks for the upper part of the walls, and a pumping system installed, Borderland had a swimming pool.

Still lined with huge stone slabs and irregular in shape, the pool is now nearing swamp-like conditions as nature reclaims the space. (Pauline A. Plimpton wrote in her *Ramblings Around Borderland* that the pool became useless after her mother died because no one else knew how to make the system work![34]) As we shall see in the next chapter, the swimming pool figured prominently in Borderland stories shared by several of the grandchildren.

34. Clark, *My Dear Mrs. Ames*, 211.

# 4

# Borderland Experiences

*"A bit of the world as it used to be"*

—Ellen Moseley Ames

ANY OF THE GRANDCHILDREN's memories of time spent with GrandB
and GrandO at Borderland involve experiences in the dining room,
at the swimming pool, and on the tennis court. Some are positive, some are
quite intimidating. Despite the passage of so many years, two of the grand-
daughters, Olivia Ames Hoblitzelle and Joanie Ames, have never forgotten
what it was like to dine with their very proper grandparents. Olivia and
Joanie insisted to me that GrandO and GrandB did not sit at the head and
foot of the dining table; they always sat amid-ships to keep an eye on the
youngsters' table manners. Then too, perhaps facing each other across the
mid-section was GrandO's and GrandB's way of signaling gender equality.
Silver goblets filled with water would be "sweating" on the table. Another
memory that stands out concerned the consequences for misbehavior, such
as the time when Olivia, sitting on her grandfather's left, put her elbows on
the table and GrandO gave her a hard whack on the elbow with the blunt
end of his dinner knife. Everyone was shocked!

Even though GrandO kept a sharp eye on misplaced elbows, the
grandchildren remember GrandB as the real disciplinarian. Grandson
Edward (Ned) Ames illustrated this with a story: Ned and his cousins had
free run of the grounds at Borderland. Ned had a frog-collecting hobby
when he was a small boy, and he suspected that there were frogs in the
icehouse. (Before refrigeration, big blocks of ice cut from ponds were
packed in sawdust in icehouses.) The icehouse door was locked, but he
could climb through a window. He dropped down onto the sawdust and

then realized he couldn't get out! He must have told his sister Olivia where he was going, because she told their father, Amyas, who came and rescued him but took him to his grandmother, who was the family disciplinarian. In her direct way, she taught him a lesson—that his curiosity was commendable, but his judgment was poor. "I got a serious talking to, not physical punishment. Her disapproval counted for a lot with me and the other kids. We were awed by her authority."

GrandO was cold and distant, Olivia recalled. "Children were not his thing. He did pay attention to my brother Ned because they shared an interest in biology." For that matter, "GrandB was not cozy or cuddly either. She was strong, really dominant. She loved lively conversation and an argument, and she had to prevail and *win* the argument." Eighty-some years later, Olivia can say, "It's fascinating to go to the house today." But at age five, when she was sick with whooping cough and was sent there to keep her from spreading it to her siblings, it was a traumatic experience and she was just plain scared of her grandmother.

Olivia's and Joanie's cousin Oakes Ames Plimpton had a similar experience. At the age of eighty-nine he can still recall the formal atmosphere of the dining room, his grandparents dressed for dinner, the servants waiting on the adults and children, and the embarrassment of having a mirror placed in front of him in an attempt to correct his unsatisfactory table manners. His sister Sarah Plimpton similarly recalled being instructed in table manners—for example, buttering one's bread the right way—and the time when a mirror was placed in front of her brother, who was a sloppy eater, and he hid behind it. Sarah's and Oakes's brother George Plimpton, the eldest grandchild, wrote in his foreword to *Jottings* that GrandO tended to remain silent at the dinner table and was known for abruptly leaving the table when he was done, though not leaving in anger. George also wrote of his puzzlement over a grandparent who could be warm and personal in letters and overly stiff and formal in person, a far cry from George's immediate family that was easy-going, gregarious, and demonstrative. Oakes was "a shadowy figure" to this grandson, especially compared to his more animated grandmother. He would "materialize" with his fancy cane beside the pool or tennis court to watch the grandchildren at play; then just as suddenly he would be gone.[1]

Oakes Ames Plimpton described his grandfather as "quite distant" and "an oddball." Grandchildren were forbidden to make noise or disturb

1. Plimpton, G., Foreword, *Jottings of a Harvard Botanist*, 28.

GrandO, especially in his study. Cousin Joanie saw their grandfather the same way but used the expression Olivia had summoned for their grandmother: he was not a "cozy" person. Joanie doesn't remember being hugged by him. She does remember his habit of impatiently drumming his fingers on the table. "I was usually an attention-seeking child, being the youngest in my immediate family, but I knew to stay under the radar when around my grandfather."

Like his older brother George, Oakes Ames Plimpton remembers his grandfather as a stickler for rules. A story involving his mother Pauline makes the point. Pauline (then a teenager) and two friends were staying with her parents at their Bay View house one August when three teen-aged boys appeared who were talking about sailing at the yacht club. That is how she and her friends became the first girl sailors at Annisquam. Pauline's catboat was red and was called Puss-in-Boots. Sailboat races started by the clubhouse at two o'clock, then went up the river and out into the sound, ending by six o'clock. On a day with absolutely no wind and a heavy tide running, Puss-in-Boots and the other little boats could make no headway. Pauline's very strict father was watching the race from a motorboat and would not let them withdraw until the race was over at six o'clock. It was a hopeless situation. They were stuck by a stone buoy at the start of the river for nearly four hours.

Grandson Oakes also described his GrandO as "puritanical, very proper" and recounted a story about his older brother for illustration. When George was playing Cole Porter tunes on the piano at Borderland, GrandO sent a maid in to tell George to stop playing "Love For Sale." This made enough of an impression on George that he mentioned it in the foreword to *Jottings*, saying he didn't know whether his grandfather disapproved of the "dubious morality of the lyrics" or simply did not want to be bothered by a grandson's awkwardness at the keyboard.[2]

According to Ned Ames, his grandfather was introverted, quiet and intense, a very different personality. GrandO would say little at the dining room table and would get up to leave when he was finished eating, regardless of the stage of others at the table. But, at other times, when alone with one of the grandchildren, "he would enter into extended and deep

2. After Harvard, George Plimpton (1927–2003) went on to become a celebrated journalist, writer, editor of the *Paris Review*, actor, amateur sportsman, and fireworks enthusiast. Several of his books detail the amusing and unique experiences he finessed as an amateur allowed to play with the New York Philharmonic Orchestra and with various professional sports teams.

conversations that always went far beyond what we had known about the subject at hand. Once when I was in my early teens, he took me for a private walk in the woods between the driveway and Leach Pond and stopped every few feet to show me another species of orchid, plants that I had never seen, or even imagined might grow in such a place. It was a generous act on his part, which revealed his deep character and interest in sharing his knowledge."

Ned saw a correlation between GrandO's reticent nature and his deliberate avoidance of the kinds of careers the men in his family typically had pursued:

> "To my recollection, my grandfather seldom talked to us about his father, Governor Oliver Ames, who had been a major figure in my family. There are extensive writings in Oakes's *Jottings of a Harvard Botanist* about how he (the professor) separated himself very consciously from pursuing a career in business, finance, or politics and focused instead on matters intellectual and academic. My generation, encouraged by our grandmother Blanche, appears to have followed his lead. My older brother (another Oakes Ames) was a physicist and a long-time president of Connecticut College, and I pursued a career in the independent sector, funding programs in science and the environment. Other members of the broader family have followed many other interests."[3]

Olivia Ames Hoblitzelle said that once she got past the trauma of being shipped off to Borderland at age five when she had whooping cough, she had happier childhood experiences in the company of her many cousins who would be sent there for two to three weeks at a time. They were free to explore and roam across the fields and meadows, ride horses, swim in the pool, and go fishing in the lake. They could pile in and drive around in a Model A Ford. Several of the teenagers learned to drive in the stripped-down old jalopy. "We weren't excited about spending time with our grandparents at Borderland—it was playing with the gang of cousins that was thrilling," Olivia recalled.

Granddaughter Sarah Plimpton described Borderland as "a paradise." She spent lots of time there with and without her cousins. Because Sarah was sick with very bad asthma as a child, GrandB decided she should sleep in a room on the top floor with nothing in it except an army cot. Sarah could hear the cousins playing outside and was able to join them for swims

---

3. Correspondence between Edward (Ned) Ames and Elizabeth Fideler.

in the pool, fishing, and canoeing on the pond. "I loved natural history and biology," she said. "GrandO certainly helped nurture my interest, but I had it anyway." Sarah added that the house in Ormond Beach, Florida was likewise "a magical place." She recalls GrandO doing a lot of fishing with her older brother George, the first of the fifteen grandchildren—and likely the favorite—on the bridge at Ormond.

Grandson Ned described Borderland as a gathering place for the extended family, many of whom came from North Easton itself or from parts of New England that were within easy driving distance. Even so, Aunt Evelyn and Uncle J. P. Davis and the four Davis cousins from Nashville, Tennessee; Aunt Pauline and Uncle Francis T. P. Plimpton and their four children from New York City; and his own parents, Amyas and Evelyn Ames and their four children, who also lived in New York City, spent considerable time at Borderland. So family gatherings tended to be large affairs, with time spent on the tennis court, in the swimming pool, and fishing and birding on the ponds. In the early days, Ned recalled, Blanche was still competitive on the tennis court, and there were frequent gatherings of friends and family from North Easton for extended tennis matches.

Ned was also able to enjoy extended visits at Borderland without his immediate family, starting before World War II and especially during his school and college years in the 1940s and 1950s, because Milton Academy and then Harvard were both within easy reach of North Easton. And when he served in the Marine Corps from 1956 through 1959 and returned on leave, Ned would go directly to Borderland. Once, coming up the front driveway from North Easton, he had to stop because of some sort of excavation in the roadway. Peering into it, he found Blanche at the bottom of the pit explaining to the contractors how to wire rebar to reinforce the concrete. She was eighty-one years old at the time.

Alex "Sandy" Walsh, a family friend, remembers Borderland well. Sandy has been a very close friend of Oliver Ames Jr. for some sixty-six years. "Ollie" and his younger brothers Angier and Thomas (the three sons of Oliver and Ellen Moseley Ames) lived next door to Sandy in Beverly Farms, Massachusetts. During the summers of 1960 and 1961when he was at the ages of fourteen and fifteen, Sandy went to visit Borderland with his age-mate Angier for a one-week stay each time. The visits were "unbelievable—an extraordinary experience!" It was great fun to spend the day fishing in a pond or driving the Model A. When it was time for lunch, they would hear the bell ringing on top of the roof. Kids from town called Borderland "The Castle," so he and Angier called it "The Castle" too, never "Borderland." There were servants, maybe six or eight, who waited on table in black uniforms with white aprons and who made the beds. "The world Blanche Ames grew up in was still alive and well in the early 1960s," Sandy said. Angier called his father's mother "GrandB," and his other grandmother (Moseley) was "Other Mummy."

The most memorable and exciting part of Sandy's first visit to Borderland was learning to drive. "For a young teenaged boy that was something!" Sandy and Angier drove the old Model A Ford along the estate's gravel and dirt roads. "It was the perfect driving school: a vast, wonderful space with no other vehicles." Many parts of the Model A had disappeared over the years, but it still had the distinctive Model A radiator grille and all the essentials— a gear shift, clutch, brake, steering wheel, and four fully inflated but well- worn tires. For Sandy, "the whole combination along with the incredible surroundings worked like a charm, and I learned to drive."

While the boys enjoyed complete freedom, GrandB did have one rule: Do *not* park the Model A in the courtyard by the front door. One day, after driving, exploring, and swimming, the boys heard the great bell at The Castle summoning them home for lunch. When Angier parked the Model A right outside the front door, Sandy reminded him about his grandmother's rule, but Angier did not listen. GrandB let the boys know she was very displeased, and they lost the use of the vehicle that afternoon and all the next day.

Sandy, too, had a Borderland swimming pool story to share. The Ames's pool, somewhat hidden behind the tennis court, was in any case not directly visible from the house. It was a hot summer day and the two boys, after cruising around in the Model A and working up a sweat, made straight for the pool. Not having their bathing suits and thinking it was private enough, they stripped off their clothes and dove into the dark, cool water, guarded only by the great bronze dragon reclining on the granite out- cropping surrounding the pool. Nevertheless, they were soon discovered.

> "Whereupon there was GrandB coming toward the pool like a dreadnought! I nervously turned toward Angier, knowing that our naked, pale bodies were impossible to hide against the black- walled pool. All of a sudden, realizing we were skinny dipping, our stern captain turned 45 degrees to starboard, sailed by, and disappeared over a rise. I detected a slight smile on her face and twinkle in her eye as she left us to our fate—drowning in sunlight

and the exhilaration of an apparent escape. GrandB was then in her eighties but in no way diminished. It was a rare experience."

Sandy's fond memories include Biscuit. "Mustn't forget GrandB's wonderful, young flame-red Irish setter. Biscuit was just like us, the incarnation of two teenaged boys enjoying the freedom of the place. He often ran alongside the Model A as we drove out of The Castle grounds, headed for some adventure, and he always welcomed us home again with innocent joy and pure enthusiasm for life. A boy's best friend."

And the library. "It was a magical, quiet place, cool and dark, lined with books," Sandy reminisced. "Just being in the library gave me an enveloping sense of ease and security." He was impressed by the various swords, including a golden ceremonial sword given by the people of General Benjamin F. Butler's hometown. The one thing about the library that was quite scary for him was the balcony that encircled the second level of the room. The balcony's floor was made of thick glass that let in light. Sandy found it unnerving to walk on its glass floor "seemingly in space," and he was terrified that the glass would break. Although he eventually conquered his fears, Sandy admitted to a lingering distrust of glass floors. (I admit to having the same reaction the first time I visited and walked tentatively around the balcony in March 2022.)

Then there was the Goodbye Ceremony. At the end of the first summertime visit, before Angier and Sandy departed from Borderland, "GrandB met us at the front door, looked me in the eye, said how much she enjoyed my visit, and did something extraordinary—she handed me sixty dollars in brand new crisp twenty dollar bills! A completely unexpected and most welcome parting gift for a teenaged boy. Of course I thanked her." The next summer, there was a similar ceremony at leave-taking but this time it was four brand new crisp twenty dollar bills, a "significant amount of money in 1964." (She did not give money either time to her grandson Angier, perhaps because he had been disobedient.) Sandy remembers buying a kit to make a diving wetsuit from neophrene and other diving equipment, such as flippers, a mask and snorkel. "I loved Jacques Cousteau, but I was too young for an aqualung."

Even though Sandy was just a young teenager when he went to Borderland, he was impressed with its grandeur. He got along very well with GrandB, whom he liked and respected. Compared to the women in his own family who were more emotional, "she was a strong, disciplined woman with a keen, very precise mind." Although these were considered more typically masculine qualities and GrandB was not a warm and cuddly person (as others have confirmed about Blanche and various family members), she "exuded a solid, reliable kindness" that Sandy found reassuring. "She bridged the gap between the genders," he noted.

At the time of those summer visits, Sandy was unaware of GrandB's many talents and accomplishments. "Although I am a painter myself and have spent many years in the art world, I do not remember discussing art with her despite my enjoyment of the paintings hung throughout the house. However, her color system and paintings came from a logical, rational way of thinking. I would say she was a stand-up woman, a woman you could count on no matter the situation. Impressive, without a doubt."

Sandy also recalled the time that he and Angier, as somewhat older teenagers, were getting ready to go to a dance at Hamilton Hall in Salem, Massachusetts when Angier's mother Ellen said to them, "I am glad you two have seen a bit of the world as it used to be." And when a friend once asked Sandy, "How does it feel to be among the elite?" Sandy could answer the gibe this way: "I am grateful for having had the opportunity to experience the world of Borderland while it was alive with the people who made it in the first place."

Yet he realized there were problems. "All the elite families had problems and had the financial wherewithal to smooth them over." Sandy was thinking of Oliver Ames (the father of his friends Ollie, Angier, and Thomas) who married late, after his naval career. Blanche's and Oakes's son Oliver was one of the few naval officers who survived the November 1943 sinking of the Casablanca-class escort carrier USS Liscome Bay near the Makin Atoll in the Pacific.[4] On what was her very first and sadly her last mission, the Liscome Bay was torpedoed by a Japanese submarine. Her bomb magazines exploded as did the fully-fueled aircraft on deck, and she sank in just twenty-three minutes: 644 men drowned, were eaten by sharks, or were horribly burned by oil. Her loss was the deadliest sinking of a carrier in the history of the United States Navy. Oliver lost the hearing in one ear but was otherwise uninjured. Three destroyers from the carrier division formation returned immediately after daylight to the area to pick up the Liscome Bay's survivors and bring them to Hawaii where they were given medical

4. The USS Liscome Bay, the flagship of Carrier Division 24 under the command of Rear Admiral Henry M. Mullinnix (who perished in the attack), had a crew of 916 and was designed to carry twenty-seven aircraft.

attention and put aboard a transport vessel that took them home.[5] Aside from his military service, Oliver never had to work. Affected by his war experience—his son Ollie suspects that he suffered from PTSD which may have worsened as he aged—he became an alcoholic, was separated from his wife, and went to live in a small apartment at the Tennis and Racquet Club in Boston. He outlived his mother merely by two years.

Sandy's own family had its share of problems as well. His father had died when Sandy was thirteen and his mother became an alcoholic. And though his family once had had a tremendous amount of wealth through shipping, finance, and railroads, it was much diminished. Like Oliver, Sandy's father never had to work. The takeaway for Sandy: "Money can be corrosive; it takes discipline to handle it properly. When the welfare child and the trust fund child are both given money, they often do not learn to do for themselves and can suffer from self-esteem problems." Professor Oakes, whom Sandy never knew, would have agreed, as evidenced by this opinion found among his *Jottings*: Harvard undergraduates of "the higher social classes" were losing out in "the race for distinction"—here he meant leadership—to those from families of moderate financial means who were willing to apply themselves industriously. In the absence of personal goals, the availability of too much wealth, even during a depression, produced shallow thinking and a lack of substance.[6]

Sandy's musings continued: "After recollecting my long ago experiences, it felt as if I were describing a time that never was and a peace-filled place that might only have been dreamed of." For that reason, he thinks the Ames biography project is extremely worthy, and he especially likes the concept of Blanche's and Oakes's partnership. "In this woefully divided, and multi-faceted world, we need an example of a married couple overcoming confusion and conflict and arriving at a state of cooperation, mutual respect, and support which worked beautifully and lasted a lifetime."

---

5. Once aboard the transport, Oliver cashed his navy paychecks so his fellow survivors would have cash to purchase supplies from the ship's store, an act of generosity described by Noles Jr. in *Twenty-three Minutes to Eternity*.

6. Ames, O. *Jottings of a Harvard Botanist*, 345–347.

# 5

# The Ameses and Woman Suffrage

*"Nothing was more important than winning woman suffrage."*
—BorderlandtheDocumentary.com

T HE FIGHT FOR WOMAN suffrage was long and hard. The woman suffrage movement was "one of the most significant and wide-ranging moments of political mobilization in all of American history."[1] According to historian Barbara F. Berenson, those in the fight " . . . had to challenge centuries of domestic tradition, church teachings, and legal doctrine that confined women to the domestic sphere and excluded them from civic participation. They lacked tools with which to seize or win power. Suffragists had to open women's eyes to their own lack of rights. They then had to persuade men, who possessed all the power, to share it. No wonder success required a campaign waged by three generations of courageous, visionary, and persistent women activists."[2]

Recognizing that activism in Massachusetts was the catalyst for the national struggle to enfranchise women, Berenson focused her work on the Commonwealth to illustrate the growing influence of the National American Woman Suffrage Association (NAWSA) and Lucy Stone's *Woman's Journal and Suffrage News* in the early twentieth century. Simply put, she wanted to give Lucy Stone (1818–1893) and her local allies the credit denied them in the suffrage narrative that has come down to us, and she felt the role of Massachusetts had been overshadowed by more successful suffrage campaigns in western states and New York State. By the late nineteenth century, Berenson pointed out, Massachusetts had become

---

1. Ware, *Why They Marched*, 8.
2. Berenson, *Massachusetts in the Woman Suffrage Movement*, 11.

the most urban state in the nation with the greatest share of its predomi-nantly immigrant population residing in cities like Boston, Fall River (to the south), Lowell (to the north), Worcester and Springfield (to the west). "Exploring suffrage from the perspective of this one state reveals both the progress and challenges in the movement in a northeastern state that had rapidly urbanized and industrialized. Studying Massachusetts also advances our understanding of the national movement."[3]

A quick tour through the nineteenth century will highlight the major players and developments shaping the movement to secure enfranchise-ment for women and provide the backdrop for the activism of Blanche and Oakes Ames.

As early as 1837 Angelina and Sarah Grimké gained fame (also no-toriety) on an anti-slavery lecture tour in Massachusetts by insisting on a woman's right to speak publicly. Lucy Stone was an ardent admirer of the Grimké sisters. Hailing from rural West Brookfield, Massachusetts, Stone saved enough from teaching jobs to enroll in Oberlin College in Ohio in 1843. Graduating in 1847, she became the very first woman from Massachusetts to earn a college degree. Because of her outstanding record, Oberlin chose Stone for a commencement address. That is, she could *write* the address but a *man* would have to deliver it, as women were banned from speaking in public. Yet, once she returned home later that year Stone embarked on the first of many paid lecture tours to speak in favor of women's rights and against slavery.

The Seneca Falls Convention in upstate New York was called in 1848 by five women seeking equal rights in marriage, education, employment, and suffrage. The best known of the five were Elizabeth Cady Stanton and Lucretia Mott, a Progressive Friend (Quaker). Some three hundred people from the area attended, most of them Quakers. All of the points contained in their "Declaration of Sentiments and Resolutions" were approved unani-mously except the resolution concerning suffrage. The Victorian notion that men and women functioned in separate spheres—domesticity for women and the civic or public domain for men—held sway. As a result, even among Seneca Falls participants the suffrage resolution seemed "a frontal attack," for it would allow women to interfere in the public sphere, and it would threaten "man's authority as sole head of household."[4]

3. Berenson, *Massachusetts in the Woman Suffrage Movement*, 95.
4. Berenson, *Massachusetts in the Woman Suffrage Movement*, 33.

Another authority on feminism and suffrage quotes an undeterred Elizabeth Cady Stanton: "We [the first generation of suffragists] solemnly vowed that there should never be another season of silence until woman had the same rights everywhere on this green earth, as man."[5] In volume one of the *History of Woman Suffrage*, co-authored in 1881 with Matilda Joslyn Gage and Susan B. Anthony, Stanton advised the next generation of young women to lead the way to their own enfranchisement, work out their own salvation with courage and determination, and, so long as the subordination of women continued, not put their trust in man since "their interests must be antagonistic."[6]

Contrary to popular belief, however, Seneca Falls was not the very first *national* convention. That honor goes to the one held in Worcester, Massachusetts in 1850 when Lucy Stone and a group of like-minded women organized The First National Women's Rights Convention, which was attended by nearly one thousand men and women from many states. Former slave-turned-abolitionist Sojourner Truth gave one of the stirring speeches. A Second National Women's Rights Convention was held the next year and attracted three thousand. Quaker reformer Susan B. Anthony attended the third convention, held in Syracuse, New York, and was so moved by Lucy Stone's speech that she decided to dedicate herself to the women's rights movement.

Throughout most of that decade, activists held more well-attended conventions on the rights of women that led to changes in state law, for example, laws allowing married women to own and sell their property and to maintain control over what they earned. Suffrage, however, remained a non-starter.

With the onset of the Civil War, campaigning for women's rights took a hiatus—during the war years, ending slavery took precedence over advancing the cause of women's rights. Passage of the Fifteenth Amendment in 1869 gave formerly disenfranchised *males* the right to vote. Lucy Stone and her husband Henry Blackwell considered it badly mistaken but did not contest it. Elizabeth Cady Stanton and Susan B. Anthony were adamantly opposed. As Berenson has pointed out, "The crack between the New Englanders and the New Yorkers [had] widened in the final weeks of 1868, when the first drafts of the Fifteenth Amendment began to circulate in

5. Dubois, *Feminism and* Suffrage, 18.

6. Dubois, *Feminism and* Suffrage, Frontispiece.

Congress.[7] Once such a deep rift opened between the two camps that year, Lucy Stone established the Boston-based American Woman Suffrage Association (AWSA); Stanton and Anthony established the New York-based National Woman Suffrage Association (NWSA) and started the organization's own newspaper called *The Revolution*.

The two NWSA leaders, Stanton and Anthony, joined forces with racist and wealthy George Francis Train in opposition to Black (male) suffrage. Stanton published polemics in *The Revolution* containing racist, classist, and xenophobic arguments against allowing the "unwashed and unlettered" to vote, for she couldn't abide the notion of non-whites and immigrants having a say in making laws for educated white women.[8]

The rival organizations would employ very different strategies. The AWSA concentrated on building support for suffrage in state legislatures and localities since it would be essential to passage of a federal amendment, while the NWSA sought influence in Congress to amend the Constitution. The AWSA also decided to pursue suffrage exclusively, despite urging from leaders of other causes, such as temperance.

By January 1870 Lucy Stone and Henry Blackwell had founded the *Woman's Journal and Suffrage News*, a Boston-based weekly newspaper, to disseminate the AWSA's views. They published speeches, debates, and convention notes concerning suffrage for women, as well as short stories, poems, and columns, and their journal became "the communications hub of the woman suffrage movement" nationally.[9] The NWSA's more radical newspaper, *The Revolution*, was short-lived and never achieved comparable prominence.

As mentioned above, in 1881 Stanton, Anthony, and Gage began what became a multi-volume but incomplete *History of Woman Suffrage*, incomplete because it almost entirely omitted Lucy Stone and her significant contributions to the movement. Largely as a result of the authors' pettiness in sidelining her work, Lucy Stone was treated like other "women of no importance" who did not receive the honor and public recognition they deserved. A massive carved marble sculpture or Portrait Monument featuring busts of Stanton, Anthony, and Mott—but not Stone—stands in the Capitol Rotunda in Washington. The absence of Stone from the widely-read,

7. Berenson, *Massachusetts in the Woman Suffrage Movement*, 50.
8. Berenson, *Massachusetts in the Woman Suffrage Movement*, 51.
9. Berenson, *Massachusetts in the Woman Suffrage Movement*, 13.

supposedly "definitive" *History* allowed the reputations of those three powerful women to overshadow her.[10]

With her mother's health failing, Alice Stone Blackwell became the editor-in-chief of the *Woman's Journal and Suffrage News* in 1890 and, along with other younger activists, succeeded in merging the NWSA with the AWSA to form the National American Woman Suffrage Association (or NAWSA). Under the leadership of Carrie Chapman Catt, the NAWSA's suffrage campaign again pursued a state-by-state strategy.

College-educated women gave the suffrage movement a much-needed boost at the turn of the century. Maud Wood Park, who graduated from Radcliffe in 1898 (one year before Blanche Ames graduated from Smith) quickly co-founded the College Equal Suffrage League, drawing on her contacts at Boston University and at the single-sex, private eastern women's colleges known as the Seven Sisters whose students were predominantly white, privileged, and Protestant.[11] For many of the earliest graduates of those institutions, the opportunity for higher education had come with a clear expectation that they would put their organizational and leadership skills to good use and contribute to the betterment of society in some way.[12] As we shall see, the message was certainly not lost on Blanche Ames Ames and Maud Wood Park—immediately after the Nineteenth Amendment secured the vote for women in 1920, Mrs. Park served as the first president of the movement's successor organization, the League of Women Voters.

Many financially secure married women joined women's clubs in the early twentieth century, some to acquire refinement via the arts, literature, and culture, some to organize "municipal housekeeping" efforts targeting public health problems and the often deplorable conditions in which the urban poor lived and worked. By 1906 having (belatedly) recognized that the movement needed buy-in from working-class women, the NAWSA formed an alliance with the Women's Trade Union League.[13] Within the

10. Three more recent biographies of Lucy Stone are: McMillan, *Lucy Stone—An Unapologetic Life*; Moore Kerr, *Lucy Stone: Speaking Out for Equality*; and Million, *Woman's Voice, Woman's Place*.

11. Gordon, *Gender and Higher Education in the Progressive Era*. (In addition to Radcliffe and Smith, the Seven Sisters were Barnard, Wellesley, Mount Holyoke, Vassar, and Bryn Mawr.)

12. Schneider, *American Women in the Progressive Era*.

13. Economist Emily Greene Balch (1867–1961) established the first settlement house in Boston, co-founded and led the WTUL to support striking workers, and later (in 1946) won the Nobel Peace Prize for her work with the Women's International League

WTUL were wage-earners' suffrage groups concerned with voting rights as well as labor union issues, such as wages, hours, and working conditions. These groups took care to point out how working-class *men* would materially benefit from women's enfranchisement.

Although the NAWSA accepted working-class women, the organization continued to exclude Black suffragists, even members of the Black women's clubs organized to fight racial and gender discrimination who could have helped to reach new audiences and advance the NAWSA's work. Mary Church Terrell (1863–1954) is a prime example. She was one of the first Black women to earn a college degree in the U.S.—like Lucy Stone many years earlier, she professed suffrage views while at Oberlin College—and went on to co-found and serve as the first president of the National Association of Colored Women, a large coalition of Black women's clubs. She was one of the few Black women to join the NAWSA after which she tried unsuccessfully to get the organization to expand membership for women of color.[14]

A small but growing number of men's groups formed to help advance the NAWSA's work. Impressed by the effectiveness of the British Men's League for Woman Suffrage, in 1909 a New York men's league began recruiting influential men with prominent names, many of whom were married to suffrage leaders. By 1910 Massachusetts had a Men's League for Woman Suffrage that was attracting sympathizers like Oakes Ames, who became a leader in the cause. These NAWSA affiliates in Massachusetts and other states—membership reached close to twenty thousand nationally—lent their support by marching in suffrage parades along with women, attending conventions, making speeches, and raising funds.

With the presidential election of 1912, woman suffrage had become a national campaign issue for the first time.[15] Woodrow Wilson had refused to support woman suffrage until his daughter convinced him otherwise: he agreed to vote in favor of New Jersey's state amendment but would not back passage of a federal amendment because, in his opinion, *states* should decide the question. Seeking to put pressure on the new president to support a federal amendment, the Congressional Union for Woman Suffrage, led by Alice Paul and Lucy Burns, sponsored a huge protest march in Washington the day

---

for Peace and Freedom and the League of Nations.

14. Chambers, "Meet the Brave but Overlooked Women of Color Who Fought for the Vote."

15. Berenson, *Massachusetts in the Woman Suffrage Movement,* 125.

before his inauguration in 1913. Paul and Burns had first-hand knowledge of the Pankhurst-led faction of militant suffragettes in England and their attention-grabbing tactics, such as picketing and hunger strikes.

Meanwhile, the more moderate NAWSA continued supporting state-level campaigns but found success only in states located west of the Mississippi River. In 1914 the NAWSA scored a major coup when the one million-strong General Federation of Women's Clubs threw its considerable weight behind woman suffrage in the belief that having the vote could enable women to achieve their municipal housekeeping goals. The NAWSA renewed its efforts to garner support: efforts included state-to-state tours featuring powerful speakers; distribution of suffrage literature, buttons, posters, and flags; fundraising; parades with bands and decorated floats; and favorable news coverage. Blanche and Oakes Ames, with the Men's League for Suffrage, were among the twelve thousand marchers who rallied at the May 3, 1914 parade in Boston.

Popular parades notwithstanding, the years 1914 and 1915 saw more setbacks for the NAWSA. A headline on the front page of the *Woman's Journal and Suffrage News* announcing "House Democrats Refuse Action" explained how a California representative's motion to create a special House Committee on equal suffrage had been defeated.[16] News from the states indicated that legislators in Massachusetts, New York, New Jersey, and Pennsylvania soundly defeated proposed constitutional amendments that would have enfranchised women.

It was commonly accepted wisdom that, if enfranchised, women would neglect their children and other domestic responsibilities. A typical front-page drawing in the *Woman's Journal and Suffrage News* advertised an upcoming talk sure to "make the audience scream with delight." With the title "How It Feels to Be the Husband of a Suffragette," it showed a self-satisfied cigar-smoking husband seated in a chair so his wife kneeling before him could put slippers on his feet and asked: "Does Suffrage 'Bust Up' the Happy Home?"[17] And men feared that, if they could vote, women would overwhelmingly approve Prohibition. Oakes Ames, as has been noted, was an exception. He was not only the husband of an ardent suffragist, he was also fully committed to the suffrage cause.

Although public opinion in many states was gradually turning toward the expansion of voting rights and the Massachusetts State Federation of

16. *Woman's Journal* (February 7, 1914) vol. 45, no. 6.
17. *Woman's Journal* (January 17, 1914) vol. 45, no. 3.

Women's Clubs, with sixty-five thousand members, lent its endorsement, the majority of men and women and the Catholic Church in Massachusetts remained decidedly *anti*-suffrage. The *Woman's Journal and Suffrage News* mocked this stance with a cartoon titled "The Anti-Suffrage Society as Dressmaker." It pictured a woman fretfully studying the outfit made by her dressmaker, a grotesque donkey-headed figure who said, "Out of date, and a bad fit? Impossible, madam! I assure you it must suit you, for I have made it exactly after your grandmother's pattern."[18]

Influenced by women in eleven western states where they could vote and prodded by the aggressive National Woman's Party (founded in 1917 by Alice Paul and Lucy Burns to replace the Congressional Union for Woman Suffrage), the NAWSA decided on a major shift in direction and began campaigning for a federal amendment. Maud Wood Park headed up NAWSA lobbying in Washington.

Between 1913 and 1915, Blanche Ames Ames supplied political cartoons to the *Woman's Journal and Suffrage News* and other local and national papers in order to help raise awareness and change public opinion about suffrage in the Commonwealth and across the country. On the *Journal's* masthead under the listing for editor-in-chief Alice Stone Blackwell, Blanche Ames Ames was listed as one of three Contributing Artists, along with subscription information (one year – $1.00, single copy – 5¢) and what today would be called a mission statement: "A weekly newspaper Devoted to Winning Equal Rights and especially to Winning Equal Suffrage for Women." The college girl who had been fiercely determined to *do something* with her artistic talents was now, in addition to illustrating orchids and other plants for her husband's various publications, creating "biting cartoons with national impact."[19]

To announce plans to expand woman suffrage in Massachusetts, New York, New Jersey, and Pennsylvania by holding referendums, the May 22, 1915 *Journal* printed Blanche's cartoon called "The Map Blossoms" on the front page. In it Uncle Sam stands beside a map of the United States, pointing pruning shears at the four states where men would decide on enfranchisement of women six months later. The word "Justice" appears on a watering can and "Equality," "Logic," "Education," and "Truth" can be seen on other gardening implements. The caption beneath the cartoon reads,

18. *Woman's Journal* (February 21, 1914) vol. 45, no. 8.
19. Crane, "Blanche Ames: Artist and Activist," 7.

"Prune away Prejudices and these four States will blossom in November."[20] Unfortunately, they did not.

NAWSA leaders had realized that they needed a new and better image of suffrage supporters, one showing them as intelligent and dignified and linking them to traditional values associated with motherhood and homemaking. Illustrations and cartoons from Blanche Ames Ames, Annie "Lou" Rogers, and Nell Brinkley, among others, presented suffragists as "young, feminine, fashionable, and independent—definitely not radical or threatening."[21] Alice Paul and Lucy Burns needed a new suffragist image for their organization too, one that would debunk anti-suffrage stereotypes by emphasizing *energetic* more than *militant*. Paul enlisted activist Nina Allender to provide cartoons for her newspaper *The Suffragist* that featured the "Allender Girl" as modern and spirited, yet respectable, the epitome of the "new woman."[22]

One of Blanche Ames Ames's most effective cartoons in the *Boston Evening Transcript* was titled "Two Pedestals." Atop the first pedestal were a graceful mother and her two little children, standing on a solid base labeled "Justice" and "Equal Suffrage," further supported by the qualities of "Motherhood, Sisterhood, Cooperation, Service, Companionship, Love," all resting on a foundation of "Education and Religion." In contrast, a second or "Anti-Suffrage" pedestal depicted an obviously disreputable woman atop a flimsy base of "Sham Chivalry" deriving from "Ignorance, Idleness, Irresponsibility, and Inferiority."[23] Anne Biller Clark's study of political cartooning on behalf of woman suffrage used "Two Pedestals" and similar drawings to make clear that Blanche was no radical feminist. "Like many moderate women, she accepted that women's right and women's duty to vote were grounded in their moral superiority as mothers, and she carefully deployed maternal images in her political cartoons supporting suffrage."[24] In fact, "she was if anything the very antithesis of the misogynist view of the woman reformer as a selfish, masculinized, denatured freak, since she worried over her children and supported her husband like any other woman."[25]

20. *Woman's Journal* (May 22, 1915) vol. 46, no. 21.

21. Berenson, *Massachusetts in the Woman Suffrage Movement*, 91.

22. Diamond, "Fighting for the Vote with Cartoons."

23. *Boston Evening Transcript* (September, 1915).

24. Clark, *My Dear Mrs. Ames*, 83.

25. Clark, *My Dear Mrs. Ames*, 159.

Another instructive Ames cartoon for the *Boston Evening Transcript* was called "The Next Rung." In it, demons labeled "Injustice" and "Prejudice" who lived in a dark pit of "Greed" and "Ignorance" thrust spears at a beautiful young woman climbing a ladder whose rungs were marked "Education," "Property," "Professions," "Business," and "Votes for Women." The demons tried to prevent her from making progress toward voting rights and "True Democracy," but she would not be deterred, no matter how difficult the climb.[26]

In a recent review of women artists from 1880 to 1940, Anna Dempsey depicts Blanche Ames as an accomplished artist, illustrator, and scientist who "did not just create outstanding art, she created art with a purpose. In Blanche's view, a painting was not just a form of creative expression, but a way to explain science, explore technique, and change American cultural and political values."[27] Her drawings effectively conveyed messages about the welfare of women generally and woman suffrage in particular by means of cartoon images that spoke to ordinary Americans. Primarily on that basis, the reviewer disputes Blanche's exclusion from the mainstream art history canon, an exclusion that both narrows our understanding of history and limits creative possibilities. "If we consider her life story, scientific achievements and political artwork, this is clearly an omission."[28]

In addition to political cartooning, Blanche's activism on behalf of enfranchisement took other forms. In 1914 Blanche served as treasurer of the Massachusetts Woman Suffrage Organization and founded and became president of the local suffrage league in Easton. Nevertheless, aside from Blanche, Oakes, and his mother Anna, the extended Ames Family was decidedly *anti*-suffrage. Oakes's sisters and their husbands and the Ames cousins contributed financially and otherwise to preventing passage of the amendment in Massachusetts.[29] Not only was the Ames Family at odds over the issue, the rest of the town of Easton was also badly divided. Historian Clark explained Blanche's non-conformity this way: "Nurtured by reform-minded parents, Blanche, unlike some other members of her class, was more willing to rock society's boat for the sake of women's rights, while most of the women of Oakes's family followed their men in taking the traditional

---

26. *Boston Evening Transcript* (November, 1915).
27. Dempsey, "Women Artists: An Untold Story," 8–9.
28. Dempsey, "Women Artists: An Untold Story," 8–9.
29. Kenneally, "Blanche Ames and Woman Suffrage," 12.

position of opposing any alteration of the status quo, a status quo which shored up their privileged lives."[30]

A prime example: Oakes's cousin Mary S. Ames of North Easton (the daughter of Frederick Lothrop Ames), who was a nationally prominent leader of the *anti*-suffrage movement. Mary S. Ames, also known as Mrs. Frothingham, particularly objected to the inclusiveness of woman suffrage, as it would allow ignorant, emotional, lower-class women to vote.[31] Starting in 1905, she was active in, then became president of, the Massachusetts Anti-Suffrage Association and vice president of The National Association Opposed to Woman Suffrage. She organized and funded the Men's Anti-Suffrage Association, a Junior Anti-Suffrage League, and the Anti-Suffrage Association of Brockton, Massachusetts. As an early anti-suffrage leader, Mrs. Frothingham engaged in all the politicking Blanche herself would soon undertake—meeting with the Massachusetts congressional delegation armed with anti-suffrage petitions, pressuring newspapers to give more coverage to the *anti* position, participating in anti-suffrage rallies, testifying against a suffrage proposal at a crowded Massachusetts legislative hearing—and, in the process, unintentionally demonstrated a woman's fitness for public speaking and politics.[32]

Putting her organizing and hosting talents to work, Blanche led a suffrage rally at Oakes Ames Memorial Hall in Easton, attended by more than seven hundred people. Her rally drew an even bigger crowd than Mrs. Frothingham's anti-suffrage rally had recently drawn at the same location. And in January of 1915 Blanche hosted a suffrage meeting and luncheon at her Borderland home. With the question of woman suffrage slated to become a ballot question on November 2, 1915, it was imperative to strategize and mobilize. The esteemed orator Maud Wood Park came to address the Borderland guests.[33] Oakes Ames described the scene this way: "I surely felt hopelessness rouse within me . . . . we thought it would be indeed remarkable if twenty people came after a storm which the papers say is the worst in the records of the Weather Bureau. So, when Blanche introduced Mrs. Park she was surprised to face nearly twice the number of people we had estimated would attend. The guests were from

30. Clark, *My Dear Mrs. Ames*, 88.
31. Kenneally, "Blanche Ames and Woman Suffrage," 7.
32. Kenneally, "Blanche Ames and Woman Suffrage," 7.
33. Friends of Borderland, "Blanche Ames, Suffrage Leader."

Brockton and the meeting was held to stimulate enthusiasm for suffrage in the social leaders of Brockton."[34]

Coverage of the event in the *Brockton Daily Enterprise* mentioned the severe winter storm and how Mrs. Ames sent motorcars to meet guests who came by trolley and carry them from the end of the line to Borderland. The guest list included the campaign leader for Plymouth County, the president and the secretary of the Brockton Equal Suffrage Association, the president of the Brockton Woman's Club, the campaign leader for Brockton, and the librarian at the North Easton Public Library. All gathered in the luxurious library at Borderland to hear Mrs. Park's address about the suffrage movement in the United States and in Australia and New Zealand where women already had the vote. The *Daily Enterprise* article continued:

> "Mrs. Park answered many questions from her audience, including some concerning the 'ignorant vote,' so-called, and showed that some of the women who are not ignorant are just the ones who need the vote. She told of the sentiment growing in the south in favor of equal suffrage because of industrial problems. The questions touched also upon divorce in suffrage States, numbers of women and men in prison in these States, industrial laws and conditions. She said that industrial conditions are not the same in Massachusetts as in Colorado and laws should not be the same. Mrs. Park emphasized the fact that each woman should not consider herself only when considering as to whether she ought to have the vote, but to consider the matter in a broad way and whether by voting she could help other women."[35]

Blanche firmly believed that for women to have economic equity in their households, married women should be able to work in a profession of their choosing. Typically, even if they were well-to-do, women who considered themselves "new women" still had to choose between having a career or a family. Poor women usually had no choice and struggled to juggle both job and family. In historian Clark's assessment, the artist's identification of suffrage with benefits to poor women in her political cartoons was more noteworthy than the many rounds of teas she gave at Borderland or her work at the polls or rallies on behalf of woman suffrage.[36] If one draws a direct line from Blanche's grandfather General Benjamin F. Butler, who used

34. Friends of Borderland, "Blanche Ames, Suffrage Leader."

35. *Brockton Daily Enterprise* (January 14, 1915), "Suffragists Hear Maud Wood Park."

36. Clark, *My Dear Mrs. Ames*, 90.

his position to champion the underdog, to Blanche, the influence of family is obvious. "Her family was privileged by education, money and rank, but it was also a family that believed in itself and in its ideas, a family that took action instead of using its wealth to fund the action of others, a family gifted in a sense of entitlement, a sense of the right to act, a sense that free speech is real and not just a constitutional issue."[37]

That mid-winter suffrage meeting at Borderland was followed by many more in the months leading up to election day in November. Despite those efforts, the ballot question that would have granted Massachusetts women the right to vote was soundly defeated. Blanche's response was a symbolic gesture: she would ring the bell that was mounted on top of the Ames mansion every day until women across the nation were enfranchised. For Blanche, "nothing was more important than winning woman suffrage." Moreover, "It wasn't political, it was personal . . . . [simply] inconceivable to her that women weren't granted the same privileges as men."[38]

We get a clear sense of Oakes Ames's strength of purpose and realistic grasp of the chances for suffrage in a letter he wrote to Mrs. Gertrude Halladay on November 1, 1918. He began by praising the "clean hard fight" she and her organization had made to secure enfranchisement, then continued with a rather emotional (for him) confidence: "I have done what I could to help, and now as the end approaches I feel that I have done too little. Should we fail to win this time it will simply be necessary to tell the opposing forces that we have just begun to fight. However, I would rather go down to defeat with the friends I admire than celebrate, with people I pity, a victory founded on injustice and won by unreason, prejudices, sophistry and deceit." The Men's League would hold a victory celebration if the vote was favorable, or they would continue the work until a celebration would be possible. "We never can be accused of being poor losers because we cannot lose."[39]

President Woodrow Wilson did back a federal amendment in 1918 in acknowledgment of women's contributions to the war effort. Yet, although the House approved the amendment, it failed to pass in the Senate. Helping to defeat it were southern Democrats and Republican senators Henry Cabot Lodge and John Weeks from Massachusetts. Blanche swung into action. The

---

37. Clark, *My Dear Mrs. Ames*, 11.

38. Friend, "Borderland—The Life and Times of Blanche Ames Ames."

39. Ames, O. Woman's Rights Collection, Folder 9. Schlesinger Library/Radcliffe Institute.

congressional committee of the Massachusetts Woman Suffrage Association, which she chaired, then targeted Weeks and succeeded in unseating him. Blanche was seen dancing with wild jubilation in the library at Borderland. Weeks's replacement, former Massachusetts governor David Walsh, was the first Democrat elected to the Senate from Massachusetts in one hundred years. That was fine with Blanche, a lifelong Republican who could see past party loyalty in this instance. And when President Wilson called a special session of Congress to consider women's suffrage, Blanche and her committee quickly mounted a massive letter-writing campaign urging the Massachusetts congressional delegation to lend its support.

The Senate finally passed the Nineteenth Amendment in June 1919. Once ratified by thirty-six states—Massachusetts was the eighth state to ratify, Tennessee the last—it became law on August 26, 1920. No doubt Blanche and Oakes would agree with Archbishop Desmond Tutu's reflections on the significance of obtaining the freedom to vote for the first time: "It's a 'cloud nine' experience. It says you *count* in your country."[40]

---

40. "On Being" host Krista Tippett's 2010 interview of Archbishop Desmond Tutu.

Blanche Ames Ames. Portrait by Edmund Charles Tarbell (1907)

Oakes Ames. Painting by Blanche Ames Ames

Borderland Mansion circa 1998. Photograph by John J. Ventresco

Blanche Ames Ames and Oakes Ames Sawing Wood at Borderland

Bell Atop Borderland Mansion

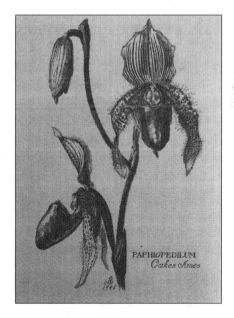

Paphiopedilum Oakes Ames

Library at Borderland

Bronze Dragon in the Library at Borderland

Blanche Ames Ames's Workshop Drawers Filled with Tubes of Oil Paints

Spool that Inspired Blanche Ames Ames's Propeller-Snaring
Invention During WWII

# 6

# Blanche Ames Ames and the Birth Control Movement

*"Every Child a Wanted Child"*
—Massachusetts Mothers' Health Council

IN ADDITION TO PAINTING portraits and drawing orchids and political cartoons, Blanche Ames Ames was the talented sculptor who carved orchids in bas-relief to adorn the sides of her husband's monument after he died in 1950. She then had the entire piece cast in bronze.[1] Another less decorous and quite audacious bit of carving took place many years earlier. When Blanche became involved in the birth control movement, it occurred to her to carve a wooden penis to use in teaching women and men how to put on a condom, even though the distribution of contraceptive information was illegal in Massachusetts. The story about the carved wooden penis circulated among Blanche's family members for years. Ames grandchildren in their eighties who repeated the story to me thought that she had demonstrated correct use of a condom at the Somerset Club, a private social club in Boston where she was a member. They also said that she was arrested on Commonwealth Avenue but was released when the policeman learned to his dismay that he had apprehended the daughter-in-law of the former governor. (Granddaughter Joanie Ames admits that she loves to tell stories—and sometimes embellishes them.)

The context for Blanche's daring act and the salacious story that was passed down within the family was a fierce determination to challenge laws restricting access to contraception. The so-called Comstock Laws (Section

---

1. The monument bearing Oakes's and Blanche's names and the names of their four children is in the cemetery of the Unitarian Church in North Easton.

211 of the U.S. Penal Code and supplements) were federal laws passed by Congress starting in 1873 that made dissemination of birth control information illegal, including by physicians; banned its transmission through the United States mail; and forbade possession of any contraceptive device, supplies, or literature. In 1879, the Massachusetts legislature passed an even more restrictive law, "Crimes Against Chastity, Morality, Decency and Good Order," prohibiting the selling, lending, giving away, or exhibiting of contraceptives. Whatever form it took, birth control was described in law as obscene, lewd, lascivious, immoral, and indecent. Violators were threatened with substantial fines and/or imprisonment. Although important changes to federal law in the 1930s made it legal for doctors to provide contraceptive information and services in most states, two states did not go along—Mississippi and Massachusetts.

Blanche took up cause of birth control after hearing the pioneering birth control advocate Margaret Sanger give a speech in Boston in 1916 in which she told the audience how her own mother had died at age fifty, after having eleven children. Mrs. Sanger's stirring oratory typically followed in this vein:

> "It is one of the anomalies of modern civilization that the forces of bigotry, reaction and legalism could so long have kept on the federal statute books a law that classed contraceptive information with obscenity and was interpreted to prevent physicians from prescribing contraceptives. Year after year this vicious law legally tied the hands of reputable physicians, while quacks and purveyors of bootleg contraceptives and 'feminine hygiene' articles and formulas flourished. It was an absurd situation in which the federal law in effect nullified the laws of practically every state."[2]

Mrs. Sanger did not coin the term "birth control" (referring to voluntary motherhood and the ability to space children), but she was the first to print it in her short-lived 1914 paper, "The Woman Rebel." The successor to "The Woman Rebel" was the journal she launched and edited from 1917 to 1928, *Birth Control Review*, a publication that gave sympathetic doctors, lawyers, clergy, artists and activists like Blanche Ames Ames a platform for news and views concerning reproductive rights.

Margaret Sanger founded the American Birth Control League (ABCL) in New York City in 1921. Women in other cities, influenced by Sanger's lecture tours and the publication of her journal, *Birth Control Review*, formed

2. Sanger, "The Status of Birth Control: 1938."

leagues in affiliation with the American Birth Control League to oppose laws restricting access to contraception, promote establishment of doctor-supervised birth control clinics like the Clinical Research Bureau Mrs. Sanger opened in 1923 in Manhattan,[3] and encourage women to control their own fertility. By 1924, the ABCL had 27,500 members.

Mrs. Sanger's organization was not the only one of its kind. The National Birth Control League, founded in 1915 by Mary Coffin Ware Dennett, promoted the use of contraception as did the successor organization Voluntary Parenthood League (VPL), started by Mrs. Dennett in 1919. Mrs. Dennett (1872–1947) was a social reformer and advocate of birth control and sex education. She wrote and published a sex education pamphlet for young people and encouraged women to take matters into their own hands by teaching their daughters *and sons* about birth control methods.

Initially a rival organization to Margaret Sanger's League, the VPL merged with the ABCL in 1925. Mrs. Sanger, who was inclined to operate as a "lone ranger," resented others in the limelight, even her own sister Ethel Byrne whose arrest in 1917 for selling contraceptive articles in New York and subsequent hunger strike in the workhouse made the headlines. Yet, she also seemed to realize the necessity for allies armed with organizing skills, useful connections, the ability to pay for legal defense, and respectable social standing.

In 1928, Mrs. Sanger resigned as American Birth Control League president and editor of the *Birth Control Review*. (The ABCL kept the journal going until 1940.) The motivation for her resignation was tactical: with the support of a newly-formed National Committee on Federal Legislation for Birth Control, she headed to Washington to wage a fight for federal legislation to permit the use of the mails for distributing contraceptives and contraceptive information. It was important to bring pressure to bear on members of the House and Senate Judiciary Committees and on Congress as a whole and to petition President Roosevelt, she told the League's leadership. (No doubt Mrs. Sanger would have been aware of Alice Paul's and Lucy Burns's redirection of the suffrage struggle in 1913 from the incremental, state-by-state approach favored by Carrie Chapman Catt and the National American Woman Suffrage Association to demands for a constitutional amendment granting suffrage to women, including National

3. Earlier, in 1916, Margaret Sanger, her sister Ethel Byrne (also a nurse), and a friend provided contraceptive information to women at a clinic in Brooklyn that was forced to close after just ten days.

Woman's Party marches, protests, lobbying, and picketing.) In 1939 the various activist organizations merged to form the Birth Control Federation of America, and in 1942, the organization became the Planned Parenthood Federation of America, the name it goes by today.

When postal authorities accused Mrs. Sanger of violating the Comstock Laws and a federal prosecutor indicted her on obscenity charges, she quickly left the country. Newspapers reporting her flight into exile before the trial inadvertently helped to spread her mantra about contraception as preventive medicine that would free women to own and control their own bodies. The publicity also helped to buttress the ranks of activists, including prominent women of means like Blanche Ames Ames, whose transition from suffrage cartoonist to birth control advocate has been aptly described as entry into "a new field of combat . . . . a logical choice for a woman determined to give to women the individuality and autonomy over their persons and their careers that had been for so long enjoyed as a male prerogative only."[4]

However, as Anne Biller Clark, a scholar of the movement, observed, "birth control was not, as suffrage had become by 1915, a respectable cause for an elite woman or for anyone else."[5] Since the cause was deemed too controversial for the National Women's Party and the League of Women Voters, Blanche would have been viewed as "something of a class renegade . . . in her support for birth control."[6] Blanche risked her reputation and social position by promoting women's reproductive rights and for challenging Catholic Church dogma on the matter. Her actions were considered outside the bounds of acceptable behavior, hardly on the border. Clark posited that Blanche's effrontery stemmed from a firm belief in social justice and a sense of entitlement linked to responsibility for others less fortunate than herself, handed down from her Butler grandfather.[7] There is no indication that her husband in any way disagreed with or disapproved of Blanche's stance vis à vis birth control—though some of his less permissive relatives no doubt strenuously objected to her advocacy—just that Oakes did not form a men's league and rally supporters for it as he had done for the enfranchisement of women.

4. Clark, *My Dear Mrs. Ames,* 123.
5. Clark, *My Dear Mrs. Ames,* 126.
6. Clark, *My Dear Mrs. Ames,* 183.
7. Clark, *My Dear Mrs. Ames,* 126.

To be fair, let's remember that during much of the time that Blanche was fighting for women's reproductive rights, Oakes was juggling multiple teaching, advising, research, writing, and administrative responsibilities all at the same time, when he wasn't traveling to far-flung locales in search of orchid specimens and books to add to his extraordinary library. "It has been said that no one individual in a lifetime association with Harvard University held more positions or was more occupied in a greater number of projects than Oakes Ames."[8] And, it should come as no surprise that the Ames's daughters Pauline and Evelyn and Blanche's sister Jessie Ames Marshall were active in Planned Parenthood. As Evelyn's son Ames Davis said to me, "Blanche's views permeated the family."

Blanche Ames Ames co-founded the Birth Control League of Massachusetts (BCLM) in 1916 with another Boston woman of similar conviction, wealth, and social position, Mrs. E. Sohier Welch.[9] Mrs. Ames was the first president and served in that capacity for nearly two decades, with one interruption. Their organization was affiliated with the American Birth Control League and maintained an office at 3 Joy Street in Boston. One of their first efforts was to join in the free speech defense of an activist who had defied Massachusetts laws banning distribution of contraceptives and contraceptive information. The activist Nils Allison was arrested, convicted, and sentenced to three years in jail for distributing a pamphlet containing the message, "Don't Have Undesired Children." Although that early legal effort to defend Nils Allison was unsuccessful, the BCLM activists were not deterred.

Over time, the BCLM created a Massachusetts Mothers' Health Council and sponsored the first Mother's Health Office, a clinic in Brookline, Massachusetts that was run by a reputable physician, in accord with the model developed by Mrs. Sanger. This represented a shift in emphasis from birth control as a free speech issue to a medical approach that would improve public health by focusing on mother and child well-being. True to her independent nature, however, Blanche disagreed with Mrs. Sanger with respect to giving *male* doctors and hospitals total control over contraception.[10] And, as we shall see, she had not changed her mind about that point when she tried to save the New England Hospital for Women and Children from male incursions some twenty years later. (See chapter 9.)

8. Schultes, in *Orchids at Christmas*, xiv.
9. Fideler, *Margaret Pearmain Welch (1893-1984)*.
10. Clark, *My Dear Mrs. Ames*, 141.

Blanche was not alone in advocating policy for keeping women, not (male) physicians, in charge of their own bodies so they could determine the number and spacing of pregnancies. The BCLM, like similar birth control leagues, attracted feminists and members who had other reasons for joining the movement, including radicals, socialists, and eugenicists seeking to limit childbearing by the physically or mentally "unfit," especially among the poor.[11] Mrs. Sanger's single-minded focus on contraception for poor women opened her to accusations of eugenics. And years later, the organization's apparent slide toward eugenics might have been the cause of Blanche ending her involvement with the BCLM. She was said to "quit in outrage" over the League's fundraising advertisement using the fact that 250,000 babies had been born to families on welfare in order to persuade taxpayers to support birth control.[12]

Eugenics was, however, an explicit aim of the Family Welfare Foundation (FWF), a short-lived initiative Blanche helped to organize in 1919. According to minutes taken at its May 21 meeting, the FWF's objectives were: "To promote the conservation of lives through rational parenthood and the welfare of mothers and children; and for this purpose, to advocate the improvement of obstetrical practice, the teaching of pre-natal and post-natal care, and the importance of eugenics in the education for parenthood."[13] Mrs. Oakes Ames was elected president. A committee of three was chosen to prepare a pamphlet for the FWF: Mrs. Ames, Dr. Young, and Mrs. East. At the September 12 meeting, Mrs. Ames moved and the members voted to appoint a committee to work out certain standards of procedures for doctors willing to cooperate with the FWF. Later the same month, the executive committee of the foundation authorized the secretary to communicate with Mrs. Mary Ware Dennett about her pamphlet "Yes-But," published by the Voluntary Parenthood League in New York City. The FWF was interested in ordering reprints of the pamphlet from the VPL, using the foundation's name and statement of objectives in place of the VPL's, and giving credit to Mrs. Dennett and the VPL. It was noted that the Massachusetts Parent-Teacher Association was "wholly in sympathy with the aims and plans of the Family Welfare Foundation" and would invite FWF speakers to go before some of the Parent-Teacher Association groups.

11. For one interpretation, see Gordon, "The Politics of Birth Control, 1920–1940," 253–277.

12. Miller, "Ames, Blanche Ames."

13. Box B–20 F, Schlesinger Library/Radcliffe Institute.

The FWF disbanded in 1920 and the trail went cold after that, at least in terms of documentation saved by Blanche, so this detour from her work with the BCLM appears to have been brief.

Greater demands on her time and attention were coming in the form of legal challenges to the Massachusetts ban on the distribution of contraceptive information. In the forefront was Dr. Antoinette F. Konikow, a physician also known for socialist leanings and radical political activism as a founding member of the Communist Party of America. As early as March 1917 Dr. Konikow was prodding Mrs. Ames. "Dear Madam," her letter began, and asked pointedly, "What has become of our Birth Control League? Is it still in existence? Have you any meetings of members?" She explained that she was anxious to hear from Mrs. Ames because she planned to lecture on sex hygiene and needed literature for distribution.[14] Dr. Konikow somehow managed to stay under the radar for a decade until she was arrested in 1928. The charge was violating Massachusetts' obscenity statutes by exhibiting articles used for the prevention of conception—she wanted women to know that a pessary called a "gold button" or a "wishbone" was a likely cause of cancer. The BCLM came to the physician's defense. For Blanche, this meant putting aside her personal distaste for the political views of the far more radical Dr. Konikow.

A February 1928 letter from Dr. Antoinette Konikow to "Interested Persons" boldly captured the situation: "The fact that a physician delivering scientific lectures before a limited audience can be arrested for discussion of birth control is an outrage possible only in Boston."[15] Contraceptive articles were sold over every drug store counter, yet a physician had no right to discuss them and point out harmful ones, she argued. "This conspiracy of silence (by the Boston papers) ought to be broken to arouse sympathizers and supporters of Birth Control to some action, which has been delayed too long." Her trial was to be that month at the Boston Court House. Punishment could be a fine from $100 to $1,000, or up to five years in state prison, or two and a half years in jail or house of correction, and loss of her medical license.

Dr. Konikow's letter and her appeal to supporters of birth control and free speech stirred the Emergency Defense Committee of the BCLM to action. The committee consisted of Mrs. Oakes Ames, president; Mrs. Jessie Ames Marshall, vice president (the BCLM president's younger sister);

14. Box B–20, Schlesinger Library/Radcliffe Institute.
15. Box B–20, Schlesinger Library/Radcliffe Institute.

Mrs. William P. Everts, treasurer; and Mrs. Edward M. East, secretary. Blanche approached several lawyers to determine their interest in defending Dr. Konikow. Mr. John P. Feeney of the firm Tyler, Eames, Wright & Hooper took the case. Blanche admitted that Mr. Feeney knew more about birth control and contraceptive methods and sales in drug stores than she did. She next approached physicians about the case and reported that those with whom she spoke were indignant about the arrest of Dr. Konikow, whom they knew to be a good physician with no complaints against her. They were in agreement that the medical profession should endeavor to have the law changed. Otherwise, every gynecologist and obstetrician would be subject to arrest. Blanche then spoke about the case on February 28, 1928 with the chairman of the State Board of Registration of Medicine, who said, "Tell her not to worry, the license won't be taken away unless she has performed abortions."[16]

Dr. Konikow was acquitted on March 1, 1928. The court said it was permissible for doctors, nurses, and individuals to give *oral* information and advice about contraception (the state still prohibited *printed* matter). The next day Mrs. Ames received a thank you note from John Feeney for having congratulated him on the successful outcome and for having sent him a spray of beautiful roses. The law firm charged $100.20 for John Feeney's services (the twenty cents was for carfare). A partner in the firm, Burton E. Eames, sent a note with the bill to Mrs. Ames the next month: "I wish, however, you would please understand that this is merely a suggestion and I should be glad to have you change the amount or tear up the bill entirely and forget it. It was a pleasure to be able to help."[17] The Emergency Defense Committee got contributions from twenty-nine individuals and expended a total of $690. Dr. Konikow returned to the lecture circuit without missing a beat. She gave a series of four talks for women only on "Sex Hygiene and Sex Problems" in January and February of 1929.

Dr. Konikow's latest work came to the attention of Mary Ware Dennett, chairman of the National Council of the Voluntary Parenthood League. Among Blanche's BCLM papers was a January 14, 1931 communication from Mrs. Dennett to the members of the National Council and the Legislative Committee. Mrs. Dennett began, "I have an item of admirable news for you." Saying she was "tempted to shout from the housetops," she wanted them to know about an "epoch-making" book on contraceptive

16. Box B-20, Schlesinger Library/Radcliffe Institute.
17. Box B-20, Schlesinger Library/Radcliffe Institute.

techniques that had been needed for so long in the United States. It was Dr. Antoinette Konikow's newest book, the *Physicians' Manual of Birth Control,* offered by the Buchholz Publishing Company for $4.00 a copy and *sold only to physicians.* (Buchholz was Antoinette Konikow's maiden name. She had published *Voluntary Motherhood: A Study of the Physiology and Hygiene of Prevention of Conception* in 1923, also a Buchholz imprint. It was reprinted five times; the last edition came out in 1938.) Here Mrs. Dennett reminded Council members with undisguised glee that while laymen would be found "criminally obscene" if they ordered the book, the law could not prevent them from *borrowing* the book from their physician. Dr. Konikow, a long-time member of the Council, was "a responsible scientific expert and an excellent educator as well." The illustrations were "a triumph of diagrammatic drawing." In Mrs. Dennett's estimation, "Nothing could form a more useful culmination to the quarter century of practical research which Dr. Konikow has given to contraceptive methods."[18]

After the exoneration of Dr. Konikow, Blanche and the BCLM were ready with their next legal challenge, "The Doctors' Bill to Clarify the Law." Its purpose was "to remove the uncertainty in the minds of physicians and their legal advisors as to whether under the existing laws physicians are restricted in giving treatment, prescriptions and instructions for the protection of health and the prevention of disease." Senate Bill 43, considering the application of Sections Twenty and Twenty-one of Chapter 272 of the General Laws affecting Physicians, Chartered Hospitals, and Medical Schools, and Standard Medical Publications, would be heard at the State House on February 18, 1931.[19]

Five days later Blanche reached out to sympathizers with the following strongly worded statement: "My Dear Fellow Citizens.... We have reached a crisis in the political and legislative activities of the state of Massachusetts .... In review of these facts, it is of no use to shut our eyes and to deny that the opposition to the bill is actuated by religious motives." With that, she zeroed in on the root of the problem, saying that she was "well aware of the gravity of raising the religious issue in a community like ours of many religions, but there is no choice in this case, because the Catholic Church has itself injected the religious issue here."[20] Under her signature Blanche

18. Box B-20, Schlesinger Library/Radcliffe Institute.
19. MC-193, Box 1, Folder, Schlesinger Library/Radcliffe Institute.
20. MC-193, Box 1, Folder 5, Schlesinger Library/Radcliffe Institute.

made sure to attest that she alone was responsible for the statements, not the Birth Control League of Massachusetts, of which she was president.

According to granddaughter Joanie Ames, Blanche did not toot her own horn but would get on her high horse and fire opinions about things she cared deeply about. At the top of the list: women should have female doctors (as was the case at the New England Hospital for Women and Children); male doctors should not have total power over women's bodies! And Joanie heard Blanche expound on the Catholic Church's position on contraception. "She was at war with the Church over birth control. She had nothing against Catholics *per se*." The staff at Borderland included Irish Catholics, Joanie knew. Still, her grandmother's opinions about the Church left young Joanie uncertain whether Catholics were "okay." On her first date with John, whom she later married, he came to the house at Cold Spring (the village in Putnam County, New York where Amyas and Evelyn and their family lived) to take her out for dinner at a Chinese restaurant. That was a bit of a novelty for Joanie: her parents did not go out to eat because they had a cook at home. When she got into John's car, she was alarmed to see two St. Christopher's medals dangling over the dashboard. In spite of GrandB's distinguishing between repudiation of the Church's ban on birth control and her acceptance of individual believers, Joanie had developed a fear of Catholics. John told her that one medal gave protection only up to speeds of 40 m.p.h. according to the Church, so he needed the second medal for higher speeds. It finally dawned on Joanie that he was pulling her leg.

In March of 1931 Blanche received another tough-minded letter from Dr. Konikow remarking on the lack of democracy in the League. "The relations between the Executive Board and the membership are so distant that the members do not know what the official policy of the organization is," the doctor observed. Nonetheless, even though she disagreed with the Executive Board, Dr. Konikow did not resign. She appeared to understand that the committee was pressed for time, owing to "the rush of work in connection with the Doctors' Bill."[21]

Needless to say, the Doctors' Bill faced an uphill battle. Legislators, courts, and public opinion in Massachusetts were all swayed by the Catholic Church's position on birth control. According to one historian, the Church had taken no official position on contraception until December 31, 1930 when Pope Pius XI issued a papal encyclical, "Casti Connubi" ("Of

21. Box B-20, Schlesinger Library/Radcliffe Institute.

Chaste Wedlock") stating that contraception was base and indecent. As a consequence, the Church explicitly prohibited Catholics from using contraception. (Pope Paul VI reaffirmed the Church's position on birth control in an August 1968 encyclical, "Humanae Vitae" ("Of Human Life"), even though the commission on birth control that he had appointed to advise him favored lifting the ban.)[22]

To reach a wider audience with her criticism of the Church's use of its authority, Blanche elaborated on the message in her "My Dear Fellow Citizens" letter in an article for the American Birth Control League's *Birth Control Review*. In "A Grave and Present Danger," which was published in the April 1931 issue, she said that the Church's teachings on contraception were unjustly affecting the lives and health of married women and their babies.

> "The long arm of the Catholic Church is reaching into our legislative halls and is directing our legislators to act according to its will .... We have all been troubled by the fear that this Catholic threat to our free institutions would materialize if Catholics were given positions of power in our government, but never before in so short a time have events developed in such irrefutable sequence as in this case of opposition to the Doctors' Birth Control Bill."

And she went on,

> "We have no quarrel with the Catholic Church and as long as it teaches its own doctrines and enforces its laws through its spiritual and moral penalties upon its own followers we, respectful as we are for all religious liberties, would not criticize it. But in the name of the same religious liberty which makes us respectful of their prejudices, we resent and protest against the use of their ecclesiastical and political influence in matters of state legislation which are not mandatory on Catholic believers. This measure is for the protection of the population as a whole which in the state of Massachusetts is still Protestant by a considerable majority."[23]

In the same issue of the *Birth Control Review*, the title page and editorial announced that the Protestant churches of America had endorsed birth control as morally justified. Speaking through its Committee on Marriage and the Home, the Federal Council of Churches of Christ in

---

22. May, (February 24, 2012). "How the Catholic Church Almost Came to Accept Birth Control—in the 1960s." See also May, *America and the Pill*.

23. Ames, B., "A Grave and Present Danger," 110–111.

America, representing the major Protestant evangelical bodies, had come to "reasoned and fearless conclusions." The Council was "unanimous in its opinion that the Catholic Church should not seek to impress its point of view with respect to the use of contraception upon the public by legislation or by any other form of coercion," and "should not seek to prohibit physicians from imparting such information to those who are entitled to it."[24]

Blanche reinforced the latter point in another article, "Permission Versus Prohibition: The Rights of Physicians to Give Contraceptive Advice in Massachusetts and a Summary of Existing State Legislation throughout the United States Concerning Physicians and the Prevention of Conception," which the Birth Control Review published in its April 1932 issue. "If physicians can be made to realize that the giving of such aid in the bona fide practice of their profession is definitely not illegal, the greatest obstacle confronting us will be removed," she declared.[25]

While Mrs. Ames and the BCLM were endeavoring to change the laws in Massachusetts, Mrs. Sanger was leading the charge in Washington, D.C. with the National Committee on Federal Legislation for Birth Control. Mrs. Sanger and her committee advanced two important reasons for amending the existing federal birth control laws that conflated birth control with obscenity. First, they argued, in a time of economic distress and unemployment (the Great Depression was causing unrelenting hardship), "Wives and mothers should be able to obtain through responsible medical channels this form of constructive relief." And second, "Increased knowledge of contraception would mean reduction in the number of criminal abortions. Over 15,000 women each year die from this cause alone." In Newsletter #12 she communicated with friends and endorsers, saying that the Senate Judiciary Committee had voted favorably on February 13, 1933 on the question of recommending Senate Bill 4436 for consideration by the full Senate. This was, she pointed out, two years from the date of the first congressional hearing on the legislation and the first recorded vote ever taken on federal birth control legislation. She then exhorted the committee's friends and endorsers: "At last we know where these men stand. Now it is for you (all capital letters made the point), who live in the states represented by the senators who voted unfavorably, to register your strong disapproval of their stand."[26]

24. Ames, B. "A Grave and Present Danger," 99.
25. Box B–20, Schlesinger Library/Radcliffe Institute.
26. Box B–20, Schlesinger Library/Radcliffe Institute.

The campaign seemed to stall after that. Margaret Sanger wrote to Mrs. Ames on letterhead of the National Committee for Federal Legislation for Birth Control, explaining that her efforts to date to attract the support of President and Mrs. Roosevelt for federal birth control legislation had been unsuccessful. She continued to hope that they would lend their support for the bill and, she imagined, if Mrs. Ames would use her influence to get them to pass on a friendly word, "it will work like magic."[27] There is, however, no evidence that Blanche had the magic touch.

Two telegrams that followed from Margaret Sanger to Blanche shed light on the slow progress made by the birth control activists. One telegram from later in January 1934 invited Blanche to lunch in Washington, D.C. and to a meeting with members of the National Committee on Federal Legislation for Birth Control. "I do not wish to impede your work but you could help tremendously," Mrs. Sanger added. Shortly thereafter on February 5, Blanche and her sister Jessie Ames Marshall met with Margaret Sanger and six members of the national committee by appointment at the Mayflower Hotel, then repaired to Mrs. Sanger's house for luncheon and to continue the conversation. They discussed the Post Office Department's decision to permit copies of *The Rhythm* to go through the mails, ostensibly because the book was not prohibited under the obscenity statutes and a lawyer's opinion that *The Rhythm* was not obscene.

Two days later Blanche sent Mrs. Sanger suggestions for dealing with *The Rhythm* problem. Blanche thought that Mrs. Sanger was justified in her disapproval of the Catholic Church's distribution of the book and in withholding her approval of the vaunted "rhythm method" until further scientific research could prove whether women are "safe" during a time each month. However, she advised, Mrs. Sanger should not stoop to using the Church's tactics (that is, employing the technical wording of the statutes) to fight, lest she appear intolerant and become the *persecutor* instead of the *persecuted*. Blanche provided publicity language that she and her sister wanted Mrs. Sanger to consider using instead. Blanche closed the letter by thanking her hostess for the opportunity to meet over lunch and tea with her and her husband, Mr. Slee.

Margaret Sanger's second telegram was sent after the Mayflower Hotel meeting and luncheon to inform Blanche that the House Judiciary Committee was unlikely to report favorably on the bill without further pressure and also to seek her help. The national committee needed

27. Box B–20, Schlesinger Library/Radcliffe Institute.

immediate action urging Chairman Hatton W. Sumners for a favorable report. Could Mrs. Ames get a hundred or more telegrams to him by Monday? Mrs. Sanger would cooperate on the expense if necessary. Presumably Blanche would have responded to this urgent request, but unfortunately we don't know the particulars.

Blanche resigned from the Birth Control League of Massachusetts in 1935. Sources claim different reasons for the decision. According to her profile in *Notable American Women*, Blanche resigned from the League in 1935 because she objected to a fundraising strategy that demeaned poor families unable to prevent pregnancies. The profile also says that she continued to press for freedom of choice, contraceptive education, and training female physicians and nurses to care for women.[28] As suggested earlier, Blanche was uncomfortable with eugenicists seeking to limit childbearing by the physically or mentally "unfit," especially among the poor. While the reader will recall her brief but active involvement with the Family Welfare Foundation in 1919, one of whose objectives was advancing eugenics when educating for parenthood, it is plausible to believe that her thinking had changed in the intervening sixteen years.

A different yet related explanation for her resignation can be found in *My Dear Mrs. Ames* where Clark posited that there were sharp differences within the membership over whether women or (usually male) physicians should be in charge of their bodies so they could determine the number and spacing of pregnancies. Blanche was against and Mrs. Sanger was for doctors and hospitals having total control over contraception.[29] "Both in spite of and because of her family," Clark said about Blanche, "she had the character and force of will to insist upon rights for women, not only for the ordinary civil rights accorded routinely to male citizens, but also for the right of women to control their own bodies and the number and timing of their births." Furthermore, "like many of her progressive generation, she sought . . . more widespread individual equality, opportunity and autonomy. She strove always at the border of the bonds that confined women of her generation, to push back the boundaries of what was respected and respectable, to extend the borders of her spiritual estate as she and Oakes had extended their lives to encompass their home and masterpiece, Borderland."[30]

28. Sicherman, *Notable American Women*.
29. Clark, *My Dear Mrs. Ames*, 141.
30. Clark, *My Dear Mrs. Ames*, 157.

Mrs. Everts, treasurer of the BCLM, announced Blanche's resignation to the membership in 1936 with an affectionate tribute to their "standard bearer" who had been steadfastly "plowing the soil and sowing the
seed" for upwards of twenty years. The lines she quoted from Walt Whit-
man captured perfectly Blanche's dedication to the cause: *Behold, I do not
give lectures or a little charity, When I give I give myself.* "I don't suppose
there is any climate more unsuited for the growth of Birth Control than
here," Mrs. Everts frankly observed. "It is sour and rugged soil and the air
is filled with raucous, bitter blasts." She said Mrs. Ames had suffered "the
vilest of abuse," citing as an example the scathing words of the district
attorney in the 1916 Allison birth control pamphlet case: "Ye female dogs,
go back to your kennels!"[31]

Mrs. Everts reminded the members about the challenges their leader
had faced in the early days, particularly gaining the cooperation of influential physicians and lawyers. Mrs. Ames had used "her charm, activity, and
light touch" effectively when instructing doctors in contraceptive technique
via demonstrations that often took place at her home. A Dr. George Gilbert
Smith credited the "high-mindedness and intelligent work of Mrs. Ames
and [her sister] Mrs. Marshall" with changing doctors' attitudes toward birth
control. And now, even though Mrs. Ames had decided to turn management over to other hands, Mrs. Everts was confident that the BCLM could
call on her help and "valiant leadership" should the BCLM "get into trouble,
be pushed off our path, [or] if there should be other arrests."

Mrs. Everts's prediction was correct. Although no longer at the
helm, Blanche continued to monitor BCLM activities and to add to her
ever-growing collection of documents about birth control, including correspondence, news clippings, the Massachusetts Mothers' Health Council
pamphlet "Every Child a Wanted Child," and other statements about the
fight for reproductive rights. Then, to no one's surprise, there were arrests
the very next year. One case Blanche followed closely involved the North
Shore Mothers' Health Office. On July 13, 1937 in the First District Court
of Essex County, Salem, Judge Sears found Dr. Lucile Lord-Heinstein and
other workers at the North Shore Mothers' Health Office guilty of breaking
a Massachusetts law against giving of contraceptive information. The judge
imposed a minimum fine of $100 on each defendant. All were released on
their own recognizance. The defendants were represented by an attorney

31. Author Elizabeth F. Fideler received a copy of Mrs. Everts's 1936 letter from
Blanche Ames Ames's granddaughter Sarah Plimpton.

for the Birth Control League of Massachusetts with which the North Shore Mothers' Health Office was affiliated.

The North Shore Mothers' Health Office was a charitable organization supported by charitable contributions, employing a duly qualified physician in charge of the medical work in the office, a registered trained nurse who assisted the physician, and two members of the association who were trained social workers working for the association without pay. The BCLM had opened the first such clinic in Brookline in 1932 and sponsored similar facilities in several other locations in the Commonwealth, believing them to be legal. Numerous medical organizations had agreed that it was sound and generally accepted medical practice to prescribe contraceptives to protect the life and health of women. As stated in a July 1937 BCLM press release: "It (North Shore Mothers' Health Office) was outstanding as the first test case in Massachusetts as to whether physicians are exempted by the courts from the literal meaning of the law as had been ruled by the Appellate Circuit Court of the Second Federal Circuit and in other states."

The most significant aspect of the trial was the testimony of three prominent physicians . . . who said that they considered contraceptive advice essential for sick women and that for years they had believed it their duty to prescribe it for their private patients to preserve health."[32] A statement from the president of the Birth Control League of Massachusetts, Mrs. Leslie D. Hawkridge (who had replaced Mrs. Ames), indicated that the ruling would be appealed because it interfered with a medical practice approved by the American Medical Association and by outstanding physicians practicing at 300 Mothers' Health Offices throughout the country.[33]

The appeal of the North Shore Mothers' Health Office case was argued before the State Supreme Court beginning in February 1938. The law said that the sale of contraceptives to married women, even on prescription of a physician and for the preservation of their life and health according to sound and generally accepted medical practice, was a crime. According to G.L. (Ter. Ed.) c. 272, Section 21, "Whoever sells, lends, gives away, exhibits, or offers to sell, lend or give away . . . any drug, medicine, instrument or article whatever for the prevention of conception" shall be punished. The defendants admitted at the earlier trial that they sold and gave away articles and medicine for the prevention of conception to various patients after a physician, with the assistance of a nurse, had examined the patients, and

32. Box 1, Folder 5, Schlesinger Library/Radcliffe Institute.
33. Box 1, Folder 5, Schlesinger Library/Radcliffe Institute.

that they were sold or given in accordance with instructions given by the physician either personally or through the nurse.

The prosecution argued that the terms of the law "are plain, unequivocal and peremptory. They contain no exceptions. They are sweeping, absolute, and devoid of ambiguity. They are directed with undeviating explicitness against the prevention of conception by any of the means specified. It would be difficult to select appropriate legislative words to express the thought with greater emphasis." The court pointed to the earliest enactment in the Commonwealth respecting the prevention of conception, echoing the language used in 1879: "In framing legislation under the police power the Legislature, without any denial of rights under either the State or the Federal Constitution, might take the view that the use of contraceptives would not only promote sexual immorality but would expose the Commonwealth to other grave dangers."[34]

Although the State of New York, in People v. Sanger, permitted physicians by statute to prescribe contraceptives under limited and defined circumstances, the court said that nothing in the circumstances of the cases at bar or in the history of the statute supported the conclusion that physicians or those acting under their instructions were intended to be excepted from the operation of the Commonwealth's statute. Therefore, the statute must be interpreted and enforced as enacted. "Exceptions overruled." The court also made clear that relief from the Commonwealth's strictures, if relief was to be had, would have to come from the *legislature* not the judiciary.[35]

The BCLM had no choice but to close all the health clinics. And, taking the court's opinion to heart, the BCLM reorganized in 1939 as the Massachusetts Mothers' Health Council and shifted the focus of its work from improving maternal and child well-being to changing the laws. After another name change, Planned Parenthood League of Massachusetts activists led state initiative and referendum campaigns in 1942 and again in 1948 to revoke the laws banning dissemination of birth control information. Despite a public education campaign to win over voters, opposition, again fueled by the Catholic Church, proved even stronger and the bills were defeated.

34. Justia U.S. Law, "Commonwealth vs. Carolyn T. Gardner. Same vs. Lucile Lord-Heinstein. Same vs. Flora Rand. Same vs. Pamelia Ferris."

35. Justia U.S. Law, "Commonwealth vs. Carolyn T. Gardner. Same vs. Lucile Lord-Heinstein. Same vs. Flora Rand. Same vs. Pamelia Ferris."

Once the ban on dissemination of birth control information was up-held, Blanche took a page from the Mary Ware Dennett playbook and recommended that women take the matter into their own hands. She encouraged mothers to teach birth control methods to their daughters. To help them, the ever-inventive Blanche created formulas for spermicidal jellies and provided instructions on how to make a diaphragm by using such everyday objects as a baby's teething ring.[36] We can surmise that it was probably around this time that she decided to carve the wooden penis.

For Blanche, taking a problem into her own hands applied as well to the childbirth experiences of her two daughters. After Pauline gave birth to her first baby in 1927, Blanche arrived from Boston and was appalled to learn that the new mother was being forced to stay in bed in the hospital for three weeks, and was scarcely allowed to put her legs over the side of the bed. Blanche had a Victrola phonograph and musical records deliv-ered to Pauline's room and hired a woman to help her daughter exercise while in bed. She also insisted that Pauline be able to nurse the baby, which meant fighting with the doctor who had insisted that formula was better for the baby than breastfeeding. Pauline did breastfeed successfully, as did Blanche's daughter Evelyn, despite a similarly fraught experience when she opted for nursing over bottle feeding for her baby.[37]

As we shall see in chapter 9, Blanche's dedication to women's repro-ductive rights came to the fore again in the 1950s when she spearheaded the campaign to save the New England Hospital for Women and Chil-dren. Nonetheless, it was not until 1966 (when Blanche was eighty-eight years of age) that the Commonwealth of Massachusetts finally amended the general laws to permit contraceptive care by prescription to married persons. Unfortunately, legalization did not eliminate strong and at times fanatical resistance to reproductive services—protesters picketing and yelling, accosting patients in the parking lot and on the sidewalk outside women's health clinics, even bombings, arson, and gunmen invading clin-ics to kill and injure staff members.

Planned Parenthood, health clinics, and women's reproductive rights are again under threat across the country as this is being written. With

36. Miller, "Ames, Blanche Ames."

37. In 1986, Pauline A. Plimpton shared her story of the "horrors" of childbirth (thirty-six hours of labor without anesthesia) in a letter to Patricia Bernstein, who was writing a book (*Having a Baby: Mothers Tell Their Stories*) about labor and childbirth as experienced by women from different eras (1890s–1990s). Patricia Bernstein's papers are part of the Sophia Smith Collection of Women's History, at Smith College.

the U.S. Supreme Court's *Dobbs* decision of June 24, 2022 to overturn *Roe v. Wade*, the landmark 1973 decision that protected a woman's constitutional right to abortion before fetal viability and after fetal viability if the pregnancy endangered the pregnant woman's life or health, many anti-abortion state legislatures have greatly restricted or banned access across the board or are trying to do so. There is even talk in some states of re-invoking the Comstock laws in order to make mailing "morning after" pills a crime—whether the recipient is an individual, a doctor's office, or a pharmacy. That could happen because the Comstock Act of 1873 has never been repealed. One can merely surmise what Blanche Ames Ames would say or do, because contraception, not abortion, was the focus of her activism. However, we do know how she felt about parent education, control over one's body, and *choice*.

It has been about one hundred years since Margaret Sanger, Mary Ware Dennett, Blanche Ames Ames and others were fighting for access to birth control methods. Melinda French Gates picked up the baton in 2012 when she saw a great need for family planning in developing countries, and she decided to prioritize contraception on her philanthropic agenda. To be able to feed and educate and care for their children, women in Asia and Africa wanted the ability to space their pregnancies and not have so many of them. Melinda French Gates said at the time, "Luckily for women in the west, it's not a life-and-death situation, but for women in the developing countries it is."[38] Sadly, the situation in the United States will have come full circle if or when women again lose control over their reproductive lives.

---

38. Moorhead, "Melinda Gates Challenges Vatican by Vowing to Improve Contraception."

# 7

# Oakes Ames's Career and
# the Ames Partnership

*"The orchid is the flower which, when it pleases,*
*pleases more than any other."*
—OAKES AMES

OAKES AMES DEVOTED HIS whole life and career to Harvard as a professor and as one of the foremost administrators in Harvard's history.[1] Having amassed the most complete collection of living orchids in
the United States in the greenhouses at The Homestead, he donated that
collection to the New York Botanical Garden[2] and turned his attention to
the study of dried specimens. In the process he became acknowledged as a
world authority on orchids and on economic botany.[3]

Although Oakes's ascent through the academic rankings to full professor in 1926 was quite slow—perhaps because he did not have a PhD—
he did not seem to mind. Having time for his scientific studies was more
important to him, and he really did not need the money. At the time of
his marriage in 1900 and until 1910 Oakes was an instructor of botany at
Harvard. After a hiatus during which he was traveling extensively, he was
appointed as assistant professor of botany in 1915. Even as an assistant
professor teaching at the Bussey Institution, he earned only a little more.

1. Vassiliki, "Oakes Ames," *American National Biography.*

2. A review of the New York Botanical Garden's 20th Annual Orchid Show (February–April 2023) says that the orchid family embraces nearly thirty thousand species on
six continents and has become the world's most cultivated horticultural crop. Heinrich,
"Celebrating the Orchid, a Botanical Superstar," C14.

3. Plimpton, P., Introduction, *Jottings of a Harvard Botanist,* 4.

Yet, according to Oakes's diary, in 1917 he was able to purchase the enormous Boston House on Commonwealth Avenue from his father's estate for $90,000.[4] (Another source says that 355 Commonwealth was owned by trusts established under his father's will and under the will of his older brother William who died in 1918, allowing Oakes to acquire the house from the trustees in 1921.)[5]

Perhaps from a sense of modesty, Oakes credited Blanche's "sublime ingenuity" with saving them from financial duress by closing off all the rooms that were not needed by the family, which included four children by then. In the sub-basement of the Boston House he installed his orchid herbarium and precious library, employed two assistants to help with the specimens, and accomplished so much that he was "dizzy" with enthusiasm. Living at 355 Commonwealth brought back wonderful memories of "youthful adventures on a glorious street." Oakes remembered holding boxing matches and practicing baseball with his friends when he was young, while the older generations would stage amateur theatricals and hold banquets, military receptions, and balls at the spacious house because his father, as governor from 1887 to 1890, was expected to host formal events.[6]

A reader of *Jottings* can only wonder how Oakes could possibly afford all the expense. The few hints of affluence lie in his somewhat breezy mention of going one year without salary owing to an oversight by Harvard and, at a later date, seriously considering leaving Harvard so he could devote his energies full time to the laboratory at North Easton. He compromised by offering to teach half time at Bussey for no pay if he could have half time for his "hobbies." President Lowell agreed to the arrangement but insisted that he be paid.[7]

As Boston's Back Bay became more built up, noise and fumes from streetcars and automobiles outside the house at the corner of Commonwealth and Massachusetts Avenues became intolerable. Oakes and Blanche decided to sell 355 Commonwealth Avenue in 1929, and they bought two equally sumptuous medieval-style houses on Bay State Road near the Charles River where the air was fresher. After the residence at 355 Commonwealth Avenue was sold, they spent a majority of their time at Borderland, their country home. It became the primary (year-round) residence

4. Ames, O., *Jottings of a Harvard Botanist*, 67.
5. Back Bay Houses, www.backbayhouses.org.
6. Ames, O., *Jottings of a Harvard Botanist*, 45.
7. Ames, O., *Jottings of a Harvard Botanist*, 94.

once they sold the house at 225 Bay State Road in 1939, although they continued to enjoy extended visits to Ormond Beach, Florida in the winter at "The Whim," the house that had belonged to Blanche's parents. The house at 225 Bay State Road became the home of Boston University's presidents for nearly thirty years and was known as "BU Castle."

Oakes was appointed to many administrative posts at the university, including chair of the division of biology; director of the Botanic Garden; curator, supervisor, and director of the Botanical Museum; supervisor of the Biological Laboratory and Botanic Garden in Cuba and of the Arnold Arboretum in Jamaica Plain; director of the Bussey Institution for Applied Biology—usually holding all those posts at the same time, not sequentially. (See chapter 8.) In 1933, at a reception for incoming Harvard president James B. Conant, Blanche heard that her husband had been on President Lowell's list of men who were qualified to succeed him, since it was known that the professor "does well anything that awakens his interest." Oakes was pleased to hear that . . . and at the same time he was very glad that it did not come to pass.[8]

Of the many institutions with which he was closely associated, Oakes was particularly invested in the Botanical Museum. The institution dated to 1858 when esteemed Harvard University botany professor Asa Gray conceived of a botanical museum modeled on London's Royal Botanic Museum at Kew Gardens, to be called the "Museum of Vegetable Products."[9] In 1923, with the museum's first director Dr. George Lincoln Goodale in very poor health, Oakes promised to "stand by" the Harvard Botanical Museum should his mentor die. Soon thereafter, Oakes was appointed curator of the institution that he deemed to be sadly neglected and well-nigh defunct.

Other than the celebrated Ware Collection of Glass Flowers, commissioned in 1886 by Professor Goodale to aid in teaching and serve as the premier botany exhibit, there was nothing to draw the interest of students or the public and no endowment with which to make improvements.[10] The Ware Collection of Blaschka Glass Models of Plants is considered one of the University's greatest treasures and is the only collection of its kind in the world. The models were made from 1887 through 1936

8. Ames, O., *Jottings of a Harvard Botanist*, 52.

9. Ames, O., *Jottings of a Harvard Botanist*, 90–92.

10. Harvard University Herbaria and Libraries, www.huh.harvard.edu. The Glass Flowers, as they are known, are exhibited in what is now the Harvard Museum of Natural History.

by Leopold and Rudolf Blaschka, father and son glass artists who lived and worked in Hosterwitz, Germany, near Dresden. Miss Mary Lee Ware, the principal funder of the collection, was from Boston and Rindge, New Hampshire, a naturalist, farmer, philanthropist, and friend of Professor Goodale and the Blaschkas. She generously made an extra donation to get improvements started, then another donor came forward to save the day. The new curator got permission to move his herbarium (then in the basement of the Commonwealth Avenue house) to the museum, in reality gifting Harvard with the Oakes Ames Herbarium and Library along with an Oakes Ames Fund for Orchidology.

The Botanical Museum today, still a center of world-wide research, consists of the Economic Botany Collections; the Economic Herbarium of Oakes Ames; the Ware Collection of Glass Models of Plants; the Paleobotanical Collection, including the Pollen Collection and the Margaret Towle Collection of Archaeological Plant Remains; the Economic Botany Library and Archives; the Archives of the Oakes Ames Orchid Library; and the Orchid Library of Oakes Ames and Herbarium. The collections are currently housed in the Harvard Museum of Natural History and the Harvard University Herbaria, which are now part of the Harvard Museums of Science and Culture or HMSC.[11]

Richard E. Schultes (1915–2001), who was mentored by Oakes Ames and in 1970 became the fourth director of the Harvard Botanical Museum, subsequently remarked on the significance of Oakes's contributions: "The academic and administrative appointments which he held over fifty years have left indelible marks on many phases of the University's biological sciences. Not the least of his accomplishments was building up the Botanical Museum toward the high level which it has attained among the world's plant science institutions."[12] Among the ways in which Oakes fostered the academic and scientific growth of the museum were: attracting a unique staff; strengthening the Paleobotanical Collection; enlarging the Laboratory of Economic Botany; transferring his personal orchid herbarium from his home to the museum and donating it to the university along with a generous endowment; and arranging for a printing press and publication of the writings and research of museum staff and students, including his own groundbreaking text, *Economic Annuals and Human Cultures*.

11. Harvard University Herbaria and Libraries, www.huh.harvard.edu.
12. Schultes, Foreword, *Orchids at Christmas*, xv.

Leslie A. Garay, who took a turn as curator of the Orchid Herbarium of Oakes Ames, provided an historical perspective on Oakes's collecting, attributing it partly to the infectious charm orchids held for the aristocracy in the Victorian period being transferred to North Easton in the New World and mostly to the collections of Oakes's father and his father's first cousin, Frederick Lothrop Ames, "a zealous cultivator" with "one of the finest collections of orchids in North America."[13] (Here Curator Garay was echoing the opinion of H. G. Reichenbach, an esteemed nineteenth-century German botanist and orchidologist.). At fifteen years of age, Oakes was collecting native orchids and adding specimens from others' collections. Already demonstrating the traits of "perfection and persistence," Garay wrote admiringly, the young man "reflected the marks of a true botanist."[14] Ten years later, Oakes's herbarium had grown along with his personal reference library, and he had joined the Harvard faculty and was publishing his research in scientific papers. The herbarium, which Garay described as a working tool for Professor Ames, "became a depository of much and varied information on orchid species in addition to the storage of dried specimens. Included were original descriptions, photographs, drawings of floral details, life-size copies of type-specimens, published plates and similar documents which would be of use for identification purposes."[15]

As mentioned in chapter 2, Oakes was beginning to be acknowledged as an expert in his field, contributing the section on orchids to the seventh edition of *Gray's Manual*, as well as writing for other scientific publications. In 1905 the Bureau of Science in Manila invited Oakes to contribute the section on orchids for a project describing the flora of the Philippines. Oakes, concerned that he did not know enough to do a good job of classifying the Philippine orchids, embarked by steamship with two assistants to study and photograph material held in London and Leiden. The year 1905 also saw publication of the first part in his seven-volume series, *Orchidaceae*. The series in its entirety would be based on his comprehensive study of the Philippine orchids and of orchids in Central America, Borneo, the United States and Canada, Peru, Guatemala, and Mexico.

Oakes and Blanche had worked together as a team from the start of their marriage. She was the artist who throughout the years made nearly all the illustrations for his *Orchidaceae* series and many other botanical

13. Garay, "The Orchid Herbarium of Oakes Ames," *Orchids at Christmas*, 41.
14. Garay, "The Orchid Herbarium of Oakes Ames," *Orchids at Christmas*, 42.
15. Garay, "The Orchid Herbarium of Oakes Ames," *Orchids at Christmas*, 42.

books and articles, working from dried or preserved specimens and bringing them to life in pen and ink drawings. Emblematic of their collaboration is a framed watercolor painting by Blanche of a hybrid orchid that was named after her husband, *Cypripedium x oakes ames.* Their son Amyas kept the watercolor in his dressing room all his adult life, and it became granddaughter Joanie's after her father died. Blanche had playfully signed her name and the date sideways along the stem of the orchid. It was September 26, 1900, the year they were married. Oakes affixed a description of the orchid and its provenance to the back of the frame. The hybrid was raised by F. Sanders and Co. and flowered in 1897 when it was exhibited in Hamburg. It was first exhibited in America at the 1900 Boston meeting of the Massachusetts Horticultural Society where it won a First Class Certificate of Merit, as did several other entries by Oakes Ames. As of 1901 no other seedling of the same cross had bloomed.

"In Oakes's diaries," their daughter Pauline commented, "he always mentions the moment when Blanche has completed a drawing. He was so interested in her work that he almost resented any distractions—children, household duties—that interrupted it."[16] In addition to illustrating Oakes's books and technical papers, in the 1920s Blanche created the phylogenetic charts of "economic" plants known as the Ames Charts. Professor Ames used the charts as teaching tools in his economic botany course, Plants and Human Affairs, widely considered as the "most original course in economic botany." We do not have to take his daughter's word for that claim, as subsequent Harvard botanists said the same thing. (In 1966 Blanche donated her husband's economic botany library collection to the Harvard Botanical Museum.) The couple also collaborated on a series of Christmas cards—Blanche doing the botanical illustrations, Oakes adding the prose and poetry—that Pauline collected for inclusion in *Orchids at Christmas.* The words and drawings in the booklet "exemplify to this daughter the extraordinary harmonization of art and science in a highly unusual husband and wife team."[17]

Blanche accompanied Oakes on many of his trips to collect orchid specimens. Early twentieth-century travel, often by donkey and on foot, to

16. Plimpton, P., Introduction, *Orchids at Christmas*, 1.

17. Plimpton, P., Introduction, *Orchids at Christmas*, 2. The booklet contains Christmas cards from 1937–1949 displaying orchid drawings by Blanche and accompanying text selected by Oakes, as well as short essays on Oakes's professional accomplishments as professor of botany and director of the Botanical Museum at Harvard from 1936–1945 and as a co-founder of the American Orchid Society in 1921.

dense, interior locations in Cuba, Central and South America, the Philippines, and Florida was surely challenging and uncomfortable, with insects, wild animals, and other hazards always a concern. Moreover, there were none of today's methods of rapid communication should help of any kind be needed. Reaching their starting point in the Yucatán, for example, was possible only by sea because there was no access by air, no rail connection to mainland Mexico, and no highway network until mid-century. According to family lore, when their car broke down during a research expedition in the Yucatán, it was Blanche who leapt out and fixed the carburetor with a hairpin and a bullet from her pistol.

Oakes decided to visit Jardim Botanica in Rio de Janeiro in 1915. He and Blanche sailed from New York on the *Vasari*, a British steamship. When they heard that the captain had lost a previous ship to German attack and saw the portholes in their stateroom painted black and closed at night, they apparently realized for the first time they might be in grave danger. Oddly enough, they had not anticipated the risk they took in crossing the ocean during World War I: their own lives could have been lost and their four children orphaned. Adopting a tone of bravado, Oakes reported that all went well on that trip, and they had a grand time on the return, too.[18]

"They were so different and had different ways of being strong, yet the marriage worked because they achieved a balance," says granddaughter Olivia Ames Hoblitzelle. Her grandfather was introverted and pathologically shy. His tall, thin, aristocratic bearing projected dignity and self-assurance, although he often came across as austere and asocial. Her grandmother was outgoing and powerful; she exhibited some of the conventionally masculine qualities. Olivia had "unbounded respect" for her paternal grandmother and admiration for her endless list of remarkable accomplishments. A proficient sportswoman who played tennis and rode horses with her husband, an expert sharpshooter who dispatched water moccasins in the Florida Everglades, an inventor—she excelled at everything she touched. In sum, "a Renaissance woman: she had so many gifts and she used them."

While Anne Biller Clark's study and some other depictions highlighted Blanche's talent for political cartooning (see chapter 5), a recent brief biographical sketch in *Harvard Magazine* argues that her greatest impact was on the scientific study of orchids, celebrating her as one of America's foremost botanical illustrators, and crediting her contributions to the study of orchidology for which Oakes is famed. He had after all

18. Ames, O., *Jottings of a Harvard Botanist*, 95.

discovered more than one thousand new species, and she was at his side for many of the discoveries.[19] "Blanche shares the credit [with Oakes] for placing orchid study on a firm scientific foundation, and not only for her incredibly precise drawings. During their fifty-year marriage, she was more than an illustrator; she was her husband's co-investigator, and he justly referred to her as his 'colleague.'"[20]

From another recent source, we get this appreciative assessment of the Ames partnership:

"As an artist, Ames is known for her drawings of orchids, which she produced over a period of fifty years to accompany her husband's groundbreaking scholarly work in orchidology. Little was known about the *Orchidicae*, one of the largest plant families, before Oakes Ames's thorough study and classification of them. In search of further identification and knowledge of orchids, Blanche traveled with her husband on expeditions to Florida, the Caribbean, the Philippines and Central and South America. Thanks to his scholarship and thousands of her minutely observed drawings, the *Orchidicae* is now the best researched and classified of all the large plant families. The Ames's cumulative work was published in the seven-volume *Orchidicae: Illustrations and Studies of the Family Orchidicae*. The couple also jointly developed the Ames Charts, using watercolors to illustrate the phylogenetic relationships of the major plants useful to humans. The charts are used to this day."[21]

*At his side, co-investigator, colleague, team, jointly developed*—the words all connote partnership. It is tempting to accept Clark's view that it was Blanche who was mainly responsible for making the relationship work so well: " . . . with her deeply sensitive husband Oakes, she succeeded in forging a lasting relationship that preserved his position in the family while according her the opportunity to act on her own beliefs. The New Woman who began by making Oakes uncomfortable, transformed herself into the gifted and companionable wife of half a century."[22] However, while it appears that she "encouraged her pessimistic husband through a lifetime of botanical work and achievement,"[23] we should not forget that Oakes was equally supportive of his wife in all her many and diverse endeavors. As

19. Snyder, "Blanche Ames—Brief Life."
20. Snyder, "Blanche Ames—Brief Life."
21. Miller, "Ames, Blanche Ames."
22. Clark, *My Dear Mrs. Ames*, 158.
23. Clark, *My Dear Mrs. Ames*, 159.

seen in chapter 3, his sincerity and devotion were evident when he wrote to Blanche from London that they had a "moral duty to standardize the other fellow's work and make life glorious where it is most keenly felt" and "to be happy, really happy, we must hold strongly to the belief in equality, and cultivate intensively that mutual ground."

As we learn from one version of a unique "lost and found" story, Oakes made sure a Brazilian orchid was named for his wife because she was the one who found it. He had heard about a rare specimen that was discovered many years earlier but was lost before it could be authenticated; a watercolor drawing that was missing essential details remained the sole clue to its existence. Lo and behold, during a research trip to Brazil with Oakes, Blanche spotted a specimen of the "lost" orchid growing on a tree, and it was named *Loefgrenianthus blanche-amesiae*.[24]

For some reason, Oakes's own telling of the orchid rediscovery story in his diary changed the details in a small but significant way. While working at the Botanic Garden in Rio de Janeiro, he and a Danish botanist named Alberto Löfgren had a conversation about orchids that they both found especially perplexing. As an example, Löfgren showed Oakes a watercolor sketch of a small-flowered Brazilian orchid that had not been seen since 1896 when it was lost or misplaced after being sent to a leading authority for identification. A few days later, on his descent from the summit of Mt. Itatiaya, Oakes spotted a single small white-flowered plant on the trunk of a fallen tree. There is no mention of Blanche when Oakes excitedly exclaimed, "I had found Löfgren's lost orchid!"[25] Only when he wrote that Löfgren named the plant in honor of Blanche did Oakes mention almost as an afterthought that *she was present* when the lost orchid was rediscovered (italics added). The truth about who made the discovery has been lost to time. Since Blanche was in fact along on the trip, perhaps she spotted the orchid on the fallen tree trunk and Oakes realized that it was the one in the watercolor sketch Löfgren showed him at the Botanic Garden. According to colleagues and students who appear in the *Jottings*, Oakes ordinarily avoided drawing attention to himself and his accomplishments, leaving one to wonder why he made himself the hero of this story.

During another trip, this one in 1922 to a herbarium in Berlin, Blanche decided to make copies of the German botanists' herbaria sheets. That proved extremely fortunate two decades later: when the bombing of Berlin

24. Miller, "Ames, Blanche Ames."
25. Ames, O., Addendum to *Jottings of a Harvard Botanist*, 400.

during World War II destroyed all the original drawings, her copies were all that was left to document the botanists' discoveries.[26]

One of the stories about Oakes that Curator Garay chose to highlight revealed the professor's talent for bringing out the best in people with whom he worked. While Oakes didn't relate well to youngsters or have much patience with them—exceptions were grandson Edward (Ned) Ames and granddaughter Sarah Plimpton who shared his love of science—he was very successful as a teacher, mentor, and colleague of scientists all around the world. (See chapter 8 for a later example of his perceptiveness.) He hired a recent Harvard graduate named Charles Schweinfurth to work in his greenhouses in 1914. Despite having one arm partially paralyzed by polio, the young man so ably tended the living orchid collection and demonstrated such remarkable powers of observation for minute detail that Professor Ames moved him to the laboratory. During a highly productive fifty-year career in orchidology, Schweinfurth became a researcher at the Botanical Museum of Harvard University, was an expert on the orchids of Peru, and was Garay's predecessor as Curator of the Orchid Herbarium of Oakes Ames.

As Garay told it, the herbarium under Oakes's oversight grew so much both in terms of *size* (sixty thousand herbarium specimens, two thousand flowers preserved in alcohol, and some eighteen thousand glycerine slides) and *value* that "serious steps had to be taken for its preservation for the benefit of the scientific world rather than the personal interest of an orchidologist-philanthropist."[27] In an act of farsightedness and generosity, Oakes donated his herbarium and specialized library of two thousand volumes in 1939 to Harvard's Botanical Museum (where in 1918 he had given his economic botanical collections), along with a fund named the Oakes Ames Fund for Orchidology whose income would cover maintenance costs and pay the salary of a curator. One condition he attached was that he would have control of the herbarium and its policies while he was alive. Blanche made a gift of a collection of her original drawings illustrating her husband's scientific writings, each of which Garay deemed "a work of art by itself." As a result, he added, "The highest quality of scholarship and the highest quality of art were truly wedded."[28]

26. Miller, "Ames, Blanche Ames."

27. Garay, "The Orchid Herbarium of Oakes Ames," *Orchids at Christmas*, 48.

28. Garay, "The Orchid Herbarium of Oakes Ames," *Orchids at Christmas*, 50.

In 1954 the herbarium was again moved to a new location, the just-completed Botany Building on Divinity Avenue in Cambridge. Garay's essay includes correspondence between Blanche Ames Ames and a Mr. R. Keith Kane for the Harvard Corporation confirming her approval and that of the family for removing the herbarium to the Botany Building *in accordance with the stipulation in the deed of the gift of Professor Ames.* Those words are italicized here because they don't line up with what is known about the controversy that first arose in 1946 when the Harvard Corporation voted to proceed with partial implementation of a plan proposed the year before by Harvard Professor of Botany I. W. Bailey. The somewhat modified form of the Bailey Plan involved removal of resources—herbarium specimens, library materials, and part of the endowment—and a substantial portion of the staff from the Arnold Arboretum in Jamaica Plain to the new Botany Building in Cambridge under the aegis of a newly created Botany Department.[29]

Curator Garay's piece in *Orchids at Christmas* devotes two pages of text on Oakes's donation of his herbarium and library to the Harvard Botanical Museum under the conditions he specified. And Garay included the June and July 1953 letters between Mr. Kane for the Harvard Corporation and Blanche stating her approval and the family's for moving the orchid herbarium to the new Botany Building in accordance with the stipulation of his deed of gift to Harvard and his herbarium and library be kept as a working unit. Arrangements to be worked out, etc. However, this 1953 correspondence does not seem to agree with the information available elsewhere, such as the pamphlet prepared by Blanche Ames and other defenders of the Arnold Arboretum in May 1958 to answer procedural and legal questions.

In addition, the 1953–1954 report by Dr. Richard A. Howard, Arboretum director at the time, said that the specimens and library books, etc. *had already been moved out of Jamaica Plain* (italics added), so it seems Blanche's approval for such a move came after the fact. One is left with questions: Did Blanche and the family agree initially to the Corporation's plan and then change their minds? Garay was full of praise for Oakes and Blanche in the

29. By the 1980s, the Orchid Herbarium contained nearly one hundred twenty-five thousand orchid specimens, a portion of them on loan from the Arnold Arboretum and the Gray Herbarium. The library had also more than doubled in size to five thousand volumes and the glycerine slides of dissected flowers exceeded twenty-five thousand. Curator Garay was proud of the fact that the Philippine and Mexican collections were "the most extensive in the world."

piece, but was he also being careful to tell the story so as not to offend his higher-ups at Harvard? Why would daughter Pauline Ames Plimpton and grandson Oakes Ames Plimpton publish something in *Orchids at Christmas* suggesting the family approved of the Corporation's plan when Blanche, Oakes's cousin John S. Ames of North Easton, and their associates clearly did not approve? John S. Ames, born in 1878 (the same year as Blanche) was the youngest child of Frederick Lothrop Ames whose outstanding collection of orchid specimens had in large part been incorporated into Oakes's own early collection. John S. Ames was angered by the diversion of those combined herbarium holdings from the Arboretum in Jamaica Plain to Cambridge, and he became the public face of the opposition forces. (See in-depth discussion of the controversy in chapter 8.)

Another tribute to Oakes and Blanche in *Orchids at Christmas* was penned by the executive secretary of the American Orchid Society, Gordon W. Dillon. Like Garay's account, Dillon's started with teenaged Oakes's passion for collecting but proceeded in a different direction. Within five years, when he was graduating from Harvard, Oakes's collection of orchid species and hybrid series cultivated in his own botanic garden was important enough to be written up in the periodical called *The Orchid Review*. Thus, in Dillon's view, with the founding of the American Orchid Society in April 1921, "it was inevitable that Oakes Ames would be among its charter members."[30] The trustees of the Society unanimously elected him vice president, and he remained in that position until his death in 1950.

When the Society's trustees proposed compiling a list of all native orchids for a Society publication, Oakes offered his own list, which was the most complete seen to that date.[31] That gesture and the list itself were considered to be typical of Oakes. By 1922 Blanche had also joined the American Orchid Society and was nominated to design a Gold Medal to be awarded at the 1924 orchid exhibition at Horticultural Hall in Boston. The Society approved her design for large and small strikings of the medal and for its seal depicting a Native American kneeling before a tree stump out of which a North American orchid grows and holding in his hand stems of South American orchids. (The model for the figure was her son Oliver, then nineteen or twenty years of age.)

30. Dillon, "Oakes Ames, Blanche Ames and The American Orchid Society," *Orchids at Christmas*, 36.

31. Dillon, "Oakes Ames, Blanche Ames and The American Orchid Society," *Orchids at Christmas*, 37.

It was also in 1924 that the Society issued *An Enumeration of the Orchids of the United States and Canada* prepared by Oakes and illustrated by Blanche. "Beautiful in format and scholarly in content, this work symbolized the gracious blend of science and aesthetics which both Oakes Ames and Blanche Ames achieved in their life with orchids."[32] They also teamed up to produce some thirty-six illustrated articles for the *American Orchid Society Bulletin* between 1932 and 1947, with the Harvard Botanical Museum housing the *Bulletin's* editorial offices. In appreciation for their many contributions, the Society honored each of them with a Large Gold Medal. And to commemorate Professor Ames's fifty years of service to Harvard University, the Society published his *Orchids in Retrospect* featuring a drawing designed by Blanche that became a gold membership pin in 1950, the year Oakes passed away.

Bringing the Herbarium story up to date is Gustavo A. Romero-González, the Venezuelan botanist, Harvard PhD, and orchid researcher who became Keeper of the Orchid Herbarium and Library of Oakes Ames in 1998. Dr. Romero-González points out that the loan and exchange of physical herbarium specimens among research institutions—customary activities for Professor Ames—are no longer commonplace. Instead, images of types and specimens of historical or diagnostic value, along with pertinent label data, descriptions, and illustrations, are available in online databases. In addition, once many countries put a stop to the collection (and theft) of biological resources and their distribution to other countries, the existing major herbaria became significant repositories for the study of plant diversity. In Dr. Romero-González's opinion, those large holdings should be considered UNESCO World Heritage sites. Furthermore, with the introduction of new scientific methods for classifying orchids and other plants, such as DNA fingerprinting, the Botanical Laboratory of Oakes Ames and his legacy "play an important role in the study of Orchidaceae in ways he never envisioned."[33]

A published "Appreciation" of Blanche's influence throughout Oakes's long career came from Richard E. Schultes after her death in 1969.[34] While Blanche never held an official appointment to the Botanical Museum staff,

32. Dillon, "Oakes Ames, Blanche Ames and The American Orchid Society," *Orchids at Christmas*, 38.

33. Romero-González, "The Orchid Herbarium of Oakes Ames Today," *Orchids at Christmas.* 52–53.

34. Schultes, "Blanche Ames Ames: An Appreciation," Box 1, Schlesinger Library/Radcliffe Institute.

she made contributions to the life of the institution that were profound: over a period of some fifty years she produced hundreds of outstanding line drawings of orchids and horticulturally important shrubs. As mentioned, she prepared the "now famous" Ames Charts of Economic Plants, four colorful wall charts depicting a phylogenetic tree that Oakes displayed to help his students interpret plant classification. Furthermore, when her husband established a printing press in the Botanical Museum in 1932 for publication of leaflets and occasional books, Blanche illustrated those publications and student and staff research papers, too. Her line drawings were widely reproduced in publications of other botanical institutions and by commercial publishers. This meant, Dr. Schultes noted, that Blanche "spent a great part of her life interpreting the beauty of plants for others."[35]

Dr. Schultes also made special mention of the portraits Blanche painted for the Botanical Museum of its first three directors, whose tenure spanned the years 1888 to 1967: Professor George Lincoln Goodale, Professor Oakes Ames, and Professor Paul C. Mangelsdorf. He ended his tribute by quoting from the eulogy delivered by the Reverend Mr. Edmund Palmer Clarke of the Unitarian Church of North Easton, "If Mrs. Ames had been a man, we would have said of her that she was 'a man of parts' . . . a person of much ability and many talents."[36]

Having earned his advanced degrees at Harvard under Professor Ames, Richard E. Schultes went on to specialize in the medicinal, economic, and industrial uses of plants, such as rubber trees, and in the uses of hallucinogenic plants by indigenous peoples in Mexico and the Amazon. After his mentor's death, Dr. Schultes became curator of the Oakes Ames Orchid Herbarium, curator of ethno-botany and executive director at Harvard's Botanical Museum, and in 1970 professor of biology. A recent review of his many accomplishments called Schultes "the archetypal Amazon explorer, the leading authority on mind-altering plants and fungi, and a founding father of rainforest conservation."[37] Among his books was *The Plants of the Gods: Their Sacred, Healing, and Hallucinogenic Powers* (1979), co-authored with the chemist who discovered LSD.

35. Schultes, "Blanche Ames Ames: An Appreciation," Box 1, Schlesinger Library/ Radcliffe Institute, 255.

36. Schultes, "Blanche Ames Ames: An Appreciation," Box 1, Schlesinger Library/ Radcliffe Institute, 255.

37. Plotkin, "Richard Evans Schultes—Brief Life," 40.

In 1979, George Ames Plimpton and his siblings Oakes and Sarah paid a visit to the Harvard Botanical Museum to see what they could learn about their grandfather from the director, whom they knew had been particularly close to Oakes. Dr. Schultes recalled for them how the extremely shy professor was nowhere to be found one time when a contingent of visiting scientists came looking for him at Harvard. He recalled the professor's mentoring of a needy student who became his apprentice and went on to make his own name in the pantheon of orchidologists, and the mentoring he himself received from Oakes that led to his own career success in botany. He enumerated Oakes's many innovations at the museum, such as changing the arrangement of the Glass Flowers exhibit from an alphabetic to a phylogenetic sequence and replacing the linotype machine with hand-set printing presses that produced finer results. What stood out for Dr. Schultes, however, was their grandfather's versatility. "He was a man of so many parts," Dr. Schultes explained. A great scientist, to be sure, and also a scholar of fine books, a businessman, a family man, head of a school committee, even a truant officer. He had strong feelings and opinions and was a man of much fuller "dimensions" than his grandson George Plimpton and his siblings had ever known.[38] They would be surprised to learn, for instance, that Oakes had a sly sense of humor that was not often revealed.

Like her Plimpton cousins, Olivia Ames Hoblitzelle had consulted Dr. Schultes some years ago on the subject of her grandfather. He told her that the professor insisted on the importance of winning the cooperation of indigenous peoples in the rainforests they visited. When doing fieldwork, "always try what's offered," Oakes would instruct Schultes and other botany students. "Trying what's offered" included the sacred and hallucinogenic plants of indigenous cultures, such as peyote. Learning this, Olivia was convinced that her grandfather would have encouraged her to try a psychoactive drug, despite its being listed as a Controlled Substance, i.e., banned in this country! Thus, years ago she and her husband Harrison "Hob" Hoblitzelle experimented a few times with LSD with a small group interested in personal growth, their inner journeys, and their spiritual development. For Olivia, the "trip" allowed her to "meet" her beloved grandfather. "I felt a deep connection to GrandO," she recalled. "I felt closer to his way of being in the world, though I am not as deeply interior a person as he was. And, given the many uncertainties of our existence today, I would give anything to have him alive right now!"

38. Plimpton, G., Foreword, *Jottings of a Harvard Botanist*, 34–35.

Olivia, a writer and teacher, was formerly associate director of the Mind/Body Clinic and a teaching fellow of the Mind/Body Medical Institute, where she did pioneering work on bringing meditation, yoga, and cognitive behavioral therapy into the medical domain to treat stress-related and chronic illness. She was also a therapist in private practice and co-director of an alternative mental health collective, as well as a hospice volunteer for many years. She is the author of *Aging With Wisdom*, a book about conscious aging, elder issues, and living the contemplative life, and *Ten Thousand Joys, Ten Thousand Sorrows: A Couple's Journey Through Alzheimer's*, a narrative memoir of how she and her husband handled his illness, drawing inspiration from their background in Buddhist practice.

Olivia described herself as an interior, contemplative, and spiritual kind of person, much like her mother Evelyn who was an author, poet, and practitioner of Transcendental Meditation.[39] As a rather quiet, inward child, Olivia wondered about many things. Even as an adult she remained as hesitant around GrandB as she had been at age five: "She [Blanche] had been an outspoken, even virulent agnostic. I was wary about getting into philosophical discussions with her, certainly not about religion, because she was formidable, articulate, and clear in her views. In truth, I respected her more than I loved her."[40] Contrast that assessment with Olivia's memories of being seven years old and watching the birds in her maternal grandmother's garden. That grandmother, Olga Flinch Perkins, or "Beep" as she was called, was from Denmark, an aging beauty who wore a crown of braids pinned up on her head. She was gentle and offered unconditional love. "Something about the sensitivity that we shared is timeless, and about how protected I felt in her presence. Most memorable was how I felt *seen* by her.... Our love for each other planted a seed for my loving old people."[41]

Olivia said that she is still coming to terms with the Ames legacy—GrandB's and her father's expectation that she should excel in all she did and "go to the top." In *Aging With Wisdom* she wrote about internalizing familial pressures to achieve, the conviction that "no matter what we do, we could always do more, or better." Indeed, her father Amyas was a managing partner at the securities firm Kidder, Peabody and Co., a member of the board of the New York Philharmonic from 1955 to 1983, and

39. When Evelyn Perkins Ames died in 1990 at age eighty-one, the *New York Times* described her as a "Portrayer of Nature in Poetry and Prose."

40. Hoblitzelle, *Aging With Wisdom*, 122.

41. Hoblitzelle, *Aging With Wisdom*, 30.

chairman of Lincoln Center from 1970 to 1980. While she shared a love of the arts with her father, he and GrandB would have wanted her to be like Hillary Clinton or Madeleine Albright.

In addition to personal revelations, *Aging With Wisdom* is filled with "wisdom treasures," i.e., "bits of information to light the way through life."[42] It provides guidelines that are indispensible to *living consciously*: 1) engage with the inner life; 2) practice silence, start the day quietly, gently to counterbalance the tendency to hurtle into action; 3) practice mindfulness and pay full attention to our ordinary activities; 4) practice stopping; 5) find the sacred in the commonplace and experience the small wonders; 6) let go of thoughts, meditate; 7) practice gratitude.[43]

Olivia thinks Oakes's insights about human behavior and the benefits of various plants remain significant, particularly with all the activity around plant-based medicines these days and the renewed interest in plants and healthy eating among younger and older men and women here and abroad. Her grandfather would have certainly appreciated authors like Michael Pollan drawing attention to the natural world, particularly psychoactive plants like opium, caffeine, and mescaline and their outsized effect on our brains and our cultures. She thinks GrandO would endorse Pollan's explanation for psychedelics' appeal to humans, that is, their ability to stimulate, calm, heal, or change consciousness, depending on the context in which they are used.[44]

42. Hoblitzelle, *Aging With Wisdom*, 52.

43. Hoblitzelle, *Aging With Wisdom*, 55–57.

44. Pollan, *This Is Your Mind on Plants* and *How to Change Your Mind*. See also: Londoño, Ernesto. "VA Is Bringing Back Experimental Therapy Using Psychedelics," A16.

# 8

# At the Arnold Arboretum

*"A museum of trees teaching the world about plants"*
—William (Ned) Friedman

For a docent-led walking tour of the Arnold Arboretum, visitors enter by the Arborway Gate at 125 Arborway, Jamaica Plain (a neighborhood of Boston), and gather near the Hunnewell Building and Visitors Center, which would reopen to the public once the COVID-19 pandemic eased. The docent leads her small group along the Meadow Road, stopping frequently to share stories and provide the name and origin of individual trees.

The docent shepherds the visitors past magnolias, lindens, horse chestnuts, maples—nothing is blooming or wearing dramatic color, as it is the end of summer. They admire the three ponds and the rosaceous collection and turn onto Bussey Hill Road, which was named for the early Arboretum benefactor, Benjamin Bussey, who donated all the land on which they were walking. Bussey was a prosperous mill owner and, like James Arnold whose bequest established and supported the Arboretum, he was a horticulturalist and philanthropist. The Bussey Institution for Applied Biology was the laboratory and research center connected with the Arboretum where Oakes Ames taught his economic botany course for graduate students doing agricultural and horticultural research.

After passing the forsythia the visitors come to the lilac allée, which will not be in its glory until Lilac Sunday in May. They learn that lilacs were among the first cultivated plants grown at the Arboretum; the oldest is a Japanese tree lilac from 1876. Moving her charges along mulch paths, the docent points out the Bonsai collection. But this is only an introductory tour. If the visitors want to see the rhododendron dell, or walnut, sweet gum, birch, beech, gingko, oak, hickory, ash, elm or crabapple trees and the Arboretum's gardens, they will have to come back another time or make a virtual visit. In just a few months, the docent is pleased to announce to the group, the Arboretum will be celebrating its sesquicentennial, which will draw much larger crowds—families, educators, students, researchers, landscape architects, nurserymen and nurserywomen eager to explore the grounds and participate in the festivities.

According to the institution's website, the Arboretum's permanent collections (which exclude nursery holdings) comprise over 15,000 individual plants that belong to 10,310 accessions. These accessions represent 2,050 different species and 1,408 cultivars, which respectively illustrate the Arboretum's broad biological and horticultural diversity, exceptional for a temperate woody plant collection. The collections are among the best documented in the world, especially with regard to wild provenance. Many of these lineages represent the original North American introductions of eastern Asian plants collected by Arboretum staff. In addition to the living collections, the Arboretum has a herbarium collection with more than 1.3 million specimens, a library of more than forty thousand volumes, and a photographic archive.[1]

After the docent recaps the early history of the Arboretum, paying special attention to its *first* director, one of the visitors (this author) asks her if she would say something about the *second* director, Oakes Ames, about whom she (the visitor) is doing research. Alas, the docent does not recognize the name.

As explained in previous chapters, Oakes Ames graduated from Harvard College in 1898, studied botany with George Lincoln Goodale, and earned his master's degree in 1899. He worked under Dr. Goodale at the botanic garden and took over as director when Goodale became head of the Harvard Botanical Museum, later to be called the Harvard Museum of Natural History. Under Goodale's influence, Oakes Ames had become interested in *economic botany*, studying plant materials as the source of products useful to mankind; for example, using trees for timber products as well as for ornamentation. As mentioned in the previous chapter, Goodale was responsible for adding the Ware Collection of Glass Flowers to the museum's holdings, and Ames assumed that responsibility when he became the museum's second director, getting flower maker Rudolf

1. Arnold Arboretum, "Collection Statistics" and "Our History."

Blaschka to create a special series of glass fruits to illustrate economic botany. Over his years on the Harvard faculty, Professor Ames taught graduate students about the taxonomy of economic plants and also gave lectures about medicinal plants to medical students. His personal Collection of Economic Botany is housed at the museum.

In 1927, Harvard President A. Lawrence Lowell tapped Professor of Botany Oakes Ames to head the university's Arnold Arboretum in Jamaica Plain following the death of the original director, Charles Sprague Sargent (1841–1927). The Arnold Arboretum had been founded in March 1872 under a bequest from the will of New Bedford whaling merchant James Arnold that specified establishment and support of an arboretum and keeping its grounds open to the public from sunrise to sunset every day of the year at no charge. Horticulture and botany were said to be "a rich man's hobby" in the late nineteenth century. Ordinary people too, particularly those living and working in crowded, dirty cities, wanted to enjoy fresh air and green space. James Arnold's bequest to Harvard and Benjamin Bussey's donation of land filled the need with an arboretum, forming "the point of intersection between science and beauty."[2]

Charles Sprague Sargent, a distinguished dendrologist (one who studies trees and other woody plants) and author, had overseen the policies and programs of the institution for well more than fifty years of its existence. "His life's purpose had been the Arboretum."[3] Early on, Sargent commissioned noted landscape architect Frederick Law Olmsted to produce a design for the Arboretum. Olmsted was also laying out a plan at the time for Boston's Emerald Necklace, a seven-mile network of graceful parks and parkways. In 1882, it was Olmsted who suggested adding the Arboretum, potentially another jewel in the necklace, to Boston's city parks system. As a result, the president and fellows of Harvard and the park commission agreed to protect the Arboretum's Jamaica Plain location for one thousand years. Under their highly unusual lease agreement, the City of Boston would own, maintain, and keep secure the grounds and hardscape—perimeter stone walls, interior roadways, gravel walks, entrance gates—and Harvard employees would be responsible for stewardship of the living collections, landscaping, and facilities.

During one of the April 2022 celebrations of the sesquicentennial of the Arboretum's founding, director William (Ned) Friedman and panelists

2. Walecki, "A Scientific Pleasure Ground," 29.
3. Hay, *Science in the Pleasure Ground*, 194.

recounted the institution's early history for an online audience numbering more than six hundred. The public-private partnership was "a unique marriage" made possible by "a remarkable coalescence of people, ideas, and philanthropy." As envisioned, the Arboretum would be "a museum of trees teaching the world about plants," unlike the other public parks controlled by the City of Boston. The speakers emphasized how Olmsted planned with the future in mind, knowing that no one would live long enough to see the young trees reach their full maturity. Generations inheriting nature's gifts—if the Arboretum was protected from development threats and commercial interests—would pass them along. What's more, Olmsted's designs were meant to be naturalistic; he considered the artificial gardens produced by mid-nineteenth-century Victorian eclecticism to be distasteful. He referred to those excesses as "gardenesque" and explained his work as landscape *architecture*, not landscape *gardening*. At first Sargent did not go along with this thinking, but he came around because he knew he needed Olmsted.[4] Moreover, the two men shared critically important values: respect for the land and respect for the visitor.[5]

The Arboretum was then and is today a 281-acre preserve " . . . devoted to scholarship and education as well as aesthetic display . . . . one of the world's centers for learning about trees and shrubs and one of the most extensive collections of hardy plants in the north temperate zone," historian of the Arboretum Ida Hay has reported. Moreover, "while increasing knowledge about the natural world was of great interest to the institution's founders, they equally valued the economic and aesthetic roles of trees in human life."[6]

One has to wonder what Oakes Ames, were he alive today, would have thought of Dr. Diana Beresford-Kroeger. The medical biochemist, botanist, author[7] and follower of ancient Celtic traditions inspired Richard Powers to base a character on her in his 2019 Pulitzer Prize-winning novel, *The Overstory*. Beresford-Kroeger was featured in the *New York Times* Science Times section for March 8, 2022 as a rather quirky but influential spokesperson

4. Best known for designing New York City's Central Park with his partner Calvert Vaux, Frederick Law Olmsted has been called "The Father of Landscape Architecture." His design for the Arnold Arboretum was the sole arboretum plan that came to fruition. Pearson, *Arnold Arboretum*.

5. Arnold Arboretum 2022 Director's Series, "Birth: The Early History."

6. Hay, *Science in the Pleasure Ground*, vii–viii.

7. See Beresford-Kroeger's *To Speak for the Trees*; *Arboretum America*; and *Arboretum Borealis*, among other titles.

for protecting the forests we have and rebuilding the ones that have been destroyed. Raised in England and Ireland in the 1940s-1950s, she imbibed Celtic medicine women's lessons in Druidic thinking that included the medicinal properties of plants and the symbiosis between plants and humans. Moving on to university science departments, she researched and verified her elders' claims about wildflowers: St. John's wort was an anti-depressant, boiled seaweed jelly could be used as an antibiotic, flavonoids in shamrocks did promote blood flow, to name a few. Today, on land she owns in Canada, Beresford-Kroeger repatriates seeds and saplings native to the region. She rhapsodizes about the ways that trees benefit our health and our souls—walking in the forest exposes one to immunity-boosting aerosols from the trees and lessens stress, she says. Equally important is their ability to absorb carbon dioxide and oxygenate the air, which makes trees our very best weapon against climate change.[8]

According to her website, "Diana's understanding of the ancient knowledge of trees has led her to unique scientific discoveries. In the 1970s Diana started her own arboretum and collected trees from all over the world. She discovered the importance of mother trees at the heart of the forest, and she scientifically proved that trees are a living library of medicine that have a chemical language and communicate in a quantum world. She created an ambitious bio-plan encouraging and educating ordinary people how to replant the global forest."[9] Professor Ames, a collector of seeds and specimens, a builder of library collections (albeit in print), and an arboretum director invested in the future would surely see in Dr. Beresford-Kroeger a kindred spirit.

When President Lowell selected Oakes Ames to head up the Arnold Arboretum after the passing of the founding director Charles Sprague Sargent, the professor wrote to tell his daughter Pauline about the appointment. Oakes was clearly aware of its significance: "I shall have the Arnold Arboretum under my wing, and the entire botanical outfit under my guidance," he explained. "At fifty-two, I have realized about as high as I can go in my chosen field of effort."[10]

President Lowell had shrewdly selected the botany professor for his diplomatic skills as much as for his scientific bona fides. He was especially charged with "bringing the Arboretum and the other independently

8. Buckley, "Her Calling: To Restore the Forests," D1, D4.
9. Beresford-Kroeger, www.dianaberesford-kroeger.com.
10. Ames, O., *Jottings of a Harvard Botanist*, 334.

endowed botanical institutions of the university into closer cohesion
. . . . "[11] The other members of Harvard's family of botanical institutions
were: the Botanical Museum; the Atkins Institution at Soledad, Cuba (an
experimental garden owned by sugar grower Edwin F. Atkins); the Gray
Herbarium; the Harvard Forest; and the Farlow Herbarium. The personal
herbarium and library of William Gilson Farlow (1844–1919), eminent
mycologist and phycologist and first Professor of Cryptogamic Botany
in North America, were bequeathed to Harvard in 1919 and formed the
nucleus of the Farlow Herbarium and Library. The Farlow Herbarium
houses approximately 1,400,000 specimens, including approximately
75,000 types of lichenized and non-lichenized fungi, bryophytes, dia-
toms and algae. It was in Professor Farlow's laboratory in Cambridge that
young Oakes Ames studied fungi in 1898 after being ejected from Latin
10 for failing a test and earned the half-credit he needed to graduate from
Harvard with his class. He could never have imagined that some thirty
years later Dr. Farlow's enormous holdings would be part of *his* extensive
and weighty portfolio of botanical institutions.

As the Arboretum's new supervisor, Oakes was aware that a longtime
employee, associate director Ernest Henry Wilson (1876–1930), had expected to be named to the top position upon Charles Sprague Sargent's
passing. E. H. Wilson was a highly experienced botanist, collector (China,
Japan, Korea, other parts of Asia and Africa), dendrologist, photographer,
and author. Ames immediately showed sensitivity and astuteness by making Wilson *keeper* of the Arboretum, a distinguished British-sounding title
he could accept.[12] And with E. H. Wilson managing many of the more demanding tasks, Ames could keep up with his professorial duties and continue collecting and writing about orchids.

Among E. H. Wilson's many publications, one in 1925 called *America's
Greatest Garden* was intended for ordinary folk who visited from all parts of
the world to view and enjoy the Arboretum's plant treasures. It was "merely a
note of invitation to a banquet of flowers and fruit provided by an assemblage

11. Hay, *Science in the Pleasure Ground*, 198.

12. E. H. Wilson was one of the foremost plant collectors of the first part of the twentieth century. British-born Wilson made multiple collecting trips to China in the early
1900s on behalf of a British firm. Under the auspices of the Arnold Arboretum he collected seeds and plants in Japan from 1911–1916, in Korea and Formosa in 1917–1918,
and from 1922–1924 in Australia, New Zealand, India, Central and South America, and
East Africa. He was appointed associate director of the Arboretum in 1919 and was made
keeper in 1927 when Oakes Ames became director.

of the world's best hardy trees and shrubs . . . . intended primarily for those who love the landscape beautiful in trunk and bark, twig and bud, flower and fruit."[13] Wilson organized the text and photographs around the seasons of the year in which certain trees and shrubs could be seen to their best advantage, with separate chapters for his favorite Arboretum walks, such as those where crabapple, lilac, azalea, rhododendron-mountain laurel, oaks, hickories, hawthorns, or conifers were to be best enjoyed.

The Arboretum had celebrated its first jubilee in 1922, Wilson noted in his book. This was during Charles Sprague Sargent's heyday and well before the Great Depression and the damaging weather events of the next decade with which Oakes Ames had to contend. The Arboretum was similar to many gardens in Europe and elsewhere that were attached to a famous university, Wilson knew. Otherwise it was "without a peer the world over."[14] What made the Arboretum extraordinary, he said, were Sargent's "untiring energy, unflinching resolve, and doggedness of purpose."[15] For the jubilee, Sargent's *The First Fifty Years of the Arnold Arboretum* described the challenges of turning a worn-out farm (the Bussey property) into a scientific garden with less than three thousand dollars a year, as well as the campaign to convince Harvard officials and the park commissioners of Boston to accept the Sargent-Olmsted plan for the Arboretum's governance. It took ten years but resulted in "the wisest and most far seeing contract of its kind that has ever been drawn up in the history of gardens for it ensures the permanency of the Arboretum in its present position for a thousand years and in all probability forever."[16]

Wilson's collaboration with Oakes Ames proved to be as smooth as it had been with Charles Sprague Sargent. They "complemented each other's abilities in the oversight of Arboretum affairs—the orchidologist set scientific and financial policies, while the keeper managed horticultural and public relations."[17] They agreed on the importance of interpreting the Arboretum and its research programs to the public, including nurserymen (growers), and horticultural clubs and societies. They welcomed pedestrian, motorized, and equestrian visitors as well as professionals from around the world who came to study the collections. Professor

13. Wilson, *America's Greatest Garden*, i.
14. Wilson, *America's Greatest Garden*, ii.
15. Wilson, *America's Greatest Garden*, 3
16. Wilson, *America's Greatest Garden*, 4–5.
17. Hay, *Science in the Pleasure Ground*, 213.

Ames encouraged interdisciplinary study of the Arboretum and widened its educational role, historian Hay noted.

In addition to having responsibility for several institutions at once during his eight-year tenure as supervisor, Oakes Ames would be faced with at least four more big challenges: the sudden death of E. H. Wilson and his wife in a car accident in 1930, the Great Depression, unusually severe winter weather in 1934 and 1935 causing serious injury to the plants, and the constant, pressing need for funds. Ames quickly started a campaign to raise one million dollars for a Charles Sprague Sargent Memorial Fund, eventually more than doubling the endowment of the Arboretum.

In a 1936 resolution published in *Science*, the American Academy of Arts and Sciences (AAAS) recognized Oakes Ames's many accomplishments as supervisor of the Arboretum, noting in particular how he "successfully maintained the traditions of the Arboretum and skillfully carried through a sound, progressive program of development."[18] By increasing the endowment, he was able to guide the institution safely through the Great Depression and even expand its scientific activities, including research in anatomy, ecology, genetics, and the pathology of woody plants. The tropical station in Cuba was added during his tenure. New greenhouses and a laboratory for plant pathology were constructed.

The 1936 AAAS resolution made particular mention of Oakes Ames's cultivation of "a warm, cooperative spirit" and his contributions to Harvard College courses. In the category of "intangibles," it was noted that Arboretum staff and co-workers "cherish the recollections of his supervisorship and our happy associations with him . . . his genial personality . . . and wise counsels . . . . "[19] These encomiums thus provide further evidence of the diplomatic skills President Lowell and his advisory board knew to be essential qualities in Charles Sprague Sargent's replacement.

Many thousands of new plants were added to the outdoor collections and the herbarium. Under Professor Ames, the Arboretum acquired roughly 15,000 specimens per year as a result of its expeditions and research projects; the library was also enlarged. In 1933 Ames described the herbarium as "one of the great botanical treasures of the world" and "an indispensable biological tool . . . for the interpretation of structure or for the investigation

18. American Academy of Arts and Sciences, "Professor Ames and Professor Jack," 200–201.

19. American Academy of Arts and Sciences, "Professor Ames and Professor Jack," 200–201.

of function."[20] Not incidentally, the herbarium was supported by an endowment provided by none other than Professor Ames himself.

Other developments under Professor Ames's supervisorship: modernizing the Arboretum's research program, broadening the scope of research in plant genetics and plant pathology (such as Dutch elm disease), and building phytopathology and cytogenetic laboratories for new hires Joseph H. Faull in forest pathology and Karl Sax in plant cytology who joined William Judd and his herbarium staff. In addition, mindful of President Lowell's charge, Professor Ames strengthened the various botanical units and encouraged more frequent interaction between Arboretum staff and Harvard colleagues—Arboretum staff regularly taught at Harvard and some advised graduate students. "It was a start to the process of coordinating the work of the Arboretum faculty with that of other Harvard botanists."[21]

When E. H. Wilson and his wife died tragically in an accident in 1930, Oakes Ames had to take on many of the late keeper's administrative responsibilities. He improved the physical condition of the grounds, widened the scope of the *Journal*, began contributing articles and photographs and his wife's botanical illustrations to Arboretum publications, and inaugurated a series of memoirs called "Contributions from the Arnold Arboretum." Unsurprisingly, this workload took a heavy toll and, tiring of it all, Ames finally asked to step down as supervisor in 1935 in order to devote more time to his orchidological studies. His replacement was Elmer Drew Merrill from the New York Botanical Garden. The university acquiesced and gave Ames a new title: Research Professor of Botany. He was then sixty-one. In the Annual Report for 1934–1935, the ninth and final report from the outgoing supervisor to the president of the university, Oakes Ames reported on the toll taken by severe winter weather as well as the overall condition and progress of the Arboretum. It was a special point of pride for him to report that he had fulfilled his charge to bring the Arboretum and the other physically separate and independently endowed botanical institutions of the university into closer cohesion.

Having shifted his attention from the cultivation of orchids to the scientific study of orchids, Ames had given most of his collection of living orchids to the New York Botanical Garden. Nonetheless, with a botanical library and herbarium of orchids in a wing of his home at Borderland, he could contentedly continue to do research, work on his books, and count on

20. Hay, *Science in the Pleasure Ground*, 205–206.
21. Hay, *Science in the Pleasure Ground*, 203.

his wife to illustrate them. *Orchidaceae* was more thoroughly documented than any other plant species as a result of their collaboration.[22]

However, the Arnold Arboretum was not to be Ames's last administrative post. He was soon called on to be director of the Harvard Botanical Museum, a position he held from 1937 to 1945, after which he took a demotion to serve, by choice, as its associate director from 1945 until his death in 1950.

Had he still been living five years later, imagine how pleased Oakes Ames would have been to learn that the Arboretum's plant cytologist Dr. Karl Sax named a "shy yet elegant" flowering crabapple tree in honor of Blanche (even though she was far from shy). We have a 1991 description of the tree from the secretary for the International Ornamental Crabapple Society Michael D. Yanny. After fifty years it had reached twenty-three feet in height and thirty-one feet in width (the proportions having changed as the tree matured) and when in full bloom created "a billowy, cloud-like impression" making it "both beautiful and unique." In fact, Yanny insisted, few trees could rival *Malus Blanche Ames* for beauty and elegance. "Yet," he continued, "even with its many superb attributes, few people know about *Blanche Ames*, and very few nurseries grow and sell the tree."[23] Among its potential landscape uses, Yanny concluded, "the graceful *Blanche Ames* overhanging a pond will create spectacular reflections when in bloom. Indeed, there are many possibilities for this fine tree, and it seems unlikely that it will remain unknown much longer. But who knows? Obscurity may be the nature of the very elegant *Blanche Ames*."[24] (Here Yanny has put a fine point on this author's thesis!)

Had he lived longer, Professor Ames would no doubt have objected to the far less savory changes that were well underway at the Arboretum in the 1950s. What became known as The Arnold Arboretum Controversy had its origins in 1945 and was not settled until 1966. For some twenty years, it was Blanche who fought the good fight in her husband's stead.

The following account of the Controversy came from Blanche and Oakes's grandson Edward (Ned) Ames in February of 2022. Ned decided to refresh his memory of the Controversy after I interviewed him for the biography and asked him questions he was unable to answer definitively. I drew his attention to Herbarium Curator Leslie A. Garay's piece in *Orchids*

22. Ruhl, "Borderland State Park."
23. Yanny, "The Shy Yet Elegant Crabapple," 33.
24. Yanny, "The Shy Yet Elegant Crabapple," 37.

*at Christmas* and to the 1953 letters between Mr. R. Keith Kane (for the Harvard Corporation) and Blanche stating her approval and the family's for moving the orchid herbarium to the new Botany Building in Cambridge. As mentioned in the previous chapter, this 1953 correspondence does not appear to be consistent with the information in the May 1958 Arnold Arboretum Committee pamphlet or with other accounts of the Arnold Arboretum Controversy. In addition, as also noted in chapter 7, a 1953–1954 report by Dr. Richard A. Howard, the Arboretum's new director, said that the specimens and library books and other material *had already been moved out of Jamaica Plain* (italics added), so it seems Blanche's approval for such a move came after the fact.

Oakes had originally accepted the Bailey Report, then questioned its legality given the terms of James Arnold's will. Three years after Oakes's death, Blanche and John S. Ames formed the Association for the Arnold Arboretum, Inc., whose 1,200 members opposed the Harvard Corporation's actions and sought to challenge them in court by means of a breach-of-trust suit. A Special Committee of seven, headed by Mrs. Oakes Ames and including a former Harvard Corporation member named Grenville Clark, outlined the Association's grievances in a statement claiming *A Denial of Justice and A Matter of Principle*. However, the Harvard Corporation, a seven-member governing body, enjoyed a degree of independence not even available to the U.S. Supreme Court—the Justices can be impeached—and did not have to answer to anyone. (Today the Harvard Corporation has thirteen members formally known as the President and Fellows of Harvard College. Its charter dates to 1650, making it the oldest corporation in the Western Hemisphere.)

The Harvard Corporation chose to ignore the findings of the Visiting Committee on the Arnold Arboretum, composed of twenty-five individuals experienced in the horticulture-botany field who were appointed by the Harvard Board of Overseers to look into the conflict. The distinguished counsel whom the Harvard Corporation hired also questioned the legality of its plan and was similarly ignored.

Many newspapers and journals covered the Controversy. A *New York Times* article on page 25 of the April 15, 1955 paper said that Harvard University was being accused of "compromising its corporate integrity as a guardian of its own sacred obligations." The Association for the Arnold Arboretum, Inc. saw this as a "breach of faith with donors and a breach of trust as a trustee for the Arboretum," thereby endangering the Arboretum as a scientific institution. In the face of these allegations, the Harvard Corporation simply maintained its silence.

Another *New York Times* article about the Controversy, this one appearing on page 140 on November 25, 1956, reported on the so-called Winterthur Statement that was issued by eminent horticulturalists and botanists attending a two-day conference on the Arboretum's losses. The conference was held in Winterthur, Delaware at the suggestion of the Association for the Arnold Arboretum, Inc. and was hosted by Henry F. du Pont. The scientists' statement said that removal of the Arboretum's materials and staff undermined its functioning and recommended that it all be returned to the Jamaica Plain location. It was not. The official explanation: Until the 1950s, all collections but the Arnold Arboretum herbarium, which was located in the Jamaica Plain section of Boston, had been housed separately in Cambridge. Upon construction of a new herbarium building on Divinity Avenue in 1954, the collections of the Gray Herbarium and Arnold Arboretum (except for cultivated plants of the Arnold Arboretum, which remained in Jamaica Plain) were brought together and integrated. The Arnold, Gray, Farlow and the Botanical Museum herbaria were thus close at hand.[25]

Here is Ned Ames's initial response to those questions:

> "What a challenge you have posed! It raises questions that I cannot easily answer, and as I have observed, there do not seem to be others in the family, or the institutions, who can help us solve the puzzle. There is no doubt about the conveyance of the Orchid Herbarium of Oakes Ames as an endowed gift to the Botanical Museum of Harvard University or about the gift of my grandmother's drawings that remain a feature of the Museum to this day. At the same time, there is no doubt that the "Controversy" took place, since it is subject of both University archives and court decisions as well as my memory. I suppose that two very different things might have occurred quite independently of each other. *Orchids at Christmas* describes the overarching, positive contributions of Oakes and Blanche and, understandably, would not have dealt with any negative or contrary events. It is possible that the Controversy was triggered by the University's mismanagement of a separate legacy of my grandfather's from the Arnold Arboretum, which was quite apart from the primary gift of the Oakes Ames Herbarium and its endowment. The timing of the events as portrayed by Curator

25. Harvard University Herbaria and Libraries, www.huh.harvard.edu.

Garay makes that interpretation challenging to imagine, but then history is seldom straightforward and one-dimensional.

Rereading *Orchids at Christmas* reminds me that a founding source of my grandfather's herbarium was the collection of his cousin Frederick Lothrop Ames, which may well have gone to the Arnold Arboretum. The John S. Ames who was Blanche's co-plaintive in the Controversy challenge was a son of Fred Ames. The diversion of Fred's herbarium would explain John's presence in the complaint.

I remember my grandmother objecting to Harvard's taking a work table favored by students at the Arnold Arboretum for its use in Cambridge and her decision to divert the planned gift of a first edition of Linnaeus that was a feature of the Borderland Library from Harvard to the University of Texas."

Once Ned's curiosity was piqued, he also took the time to seek help from archivists at Harvard University. The archived collection concerning the legal Controversy contains correspondence, along with published and unpublished documents including journal articles, brochures, reprints, reports, pamphlets, photographs, and newspaper clippings. The records include: The Bailey Report; Arnold Arboretum Visiting Committee; The Association for the Arnold Arboretum, Inc.; Opposition to the Bailey Plan; and Massachusetts Supreme Judicial Court Documents. Dr. Richard A. Howard, Arnold Professor and director of the Arnold Arboretum from 1954 to 1978, compiled and assembled most of the reference material.[26]

Here is what Ned Ames's further research into the Controversy turned up:

> "The following is an internal document that I prepared to bring my memories of discussions with my grandmother, Blanche Ames, into line with what I have learned since, and to provide information for Elizabeth Fideler, who is writing Blanche's biography. I was present for some of the later events described below, first at my grandmother's table, and then both as a student at Harvard majoring in biology in the 1950s and as a member of a visiting committee appointed by the Biology Department in the 1970s. In the case of conflicting memories, I have sided

26. "The Controversy" Records, 1945–1966: Guide, www.arboretum.harvard.edu. See also Arnold Arboretum Library. Dr. Howard began his Harvard career working under I. W. Bailey in 1938, earned his doctorate in botany in 1942, then joined the Biology Department as an assistant professor and Arboretum staff member until 1953, after which he served as the Arboretum's director.

with the archives, and I am indebted to Danielle Castronovo and Gretchen Wade of the Harvard University Herbaria and Libraries for guiding me through them.

My grandfather, Professor Oakes Ames, was supervisor of the Arnold Arboretum from 1927–1935 and chairman of Harvard's Division of Biology from 1926–1935. In 1946 Harvard issued a report known as the Bailey Plan, named after its author, Professor Irving W. Bailey. The Plan, which was not immediately implemented at the time, would have moved the Arboretum's herbarium, books and botanical records from Jamaica Plain, where the Arboretum is located, to a new centralized building in Cambridge. Allegedly, it would have also taken over the endowment intended for the support of the Arboretum's collections.

Oakes initially accepted the Bailey Plan, but by 1949 he was increasingly concerned about Harvard's management of the Arboretum, and he raised questions about the legality of the University's taking over the endowment. Oakes died in 1950 with his questions unanswered.

In 1953 the Harvard Board of Overseers voted to set aside the Bailey Plan, which contained controversial ideas, but, at the same time, the Overseers authorized transferring a major portion of the Arboretum's books and herbarium specimens to Cambridge, along with a portion of its endowment. The Arboretum, founded in 1872, had an endowment of five million dollars in 1954 that produced some two hundred thousand dollars a year to support its collections. The reasons given by the Overseers for the move included the overcrowding of the Arboretum's administrative building in Jamaica Plain, a lack of space for display cases and herbarium boxes, and inadequate library space that resulted in limited access to its books. More fundamentally, there were financial concerns about the University's position in supporting two separate programs in the same field. The University completed the transfers to Cambridge in 1954, placing the collections in what was later named the Harvard University Herbaria.

Since Oakes had been the originator of many of the books, herbarium sheets, and other materials at the Arboretum, Blanche was obviously concerned. Following the 1953 Board of Overseers decision, a group of people interested in the Arboretum founded a citizen's public interest group called The Association for the Arnold Arboretum, Inc. The Association was entirely independent of Harvard University and had no legal relationship with the Arboretum. Blanche, as Oakes's widow, along with Oakes's cousin

John S. Ames from North Easton, Massachusetts, were dominant members of its board.

Blanche became a member of a special committee of the Association that applied to the Massachusetts Attorney General for a so-called 'relators suit' in which the Attorney General would be asked to act for the complainants, since they would have no standing under State law to act on their own behalf. The committee alleged a breach of trust by Harvard in its management of endowment funds. Harvard opposed the bringing of such an action, and the committee sued directly, but was unsuccessful in overcoming the opposition of the University.

The Association published a statement in 1956 entitled *A Denial of Justice and a Matter of Principle*. The statement, which was signed by Blanche and her colleagues on the special committee, detailed their charges against the University and accused it of secretly blocking their request for a review by the Attorney General. The distribution of the statement in brochure form attracted extensive publicity, both within the University community and nationally through the press.

The challenge by the Association was disruptive, and Blanche was seen as its architect. In 1952, when I was a student at Harvard majoring in biology, Professor Paul C. Mangelsdorf called me to the head of the lecture hall (he did not know me), and asked me to approach my grandmother to persuade her to drop her case against the University. I remained silent, and he dropped the subject. In 1953, when Nathan Pusey became president of Harvard, I was told that when he learned of the dispute and realized the weakness of the University's position, he ordered a settlement granting my grandmother's wishes. That settlement never happened, and the story must have been apocryphal.

The "Controversy," as it became known, continued with a series of actions involving the Attorney General's office, and was pursued with the aid of prominent Boston lawyers Robert G. Dodge and J. W. Farley, while Oscar Shaw of Ropes and Gray represented the University. In 1958 a newly elected Attorney General, Edward J. McCormack Jr., was convinced enough by the Association's allegations to bring a lawsuit in his name against Harvard. That suit was not resolved until 1966 when the Massachusetts Supreme Judicial Court voted 3–2 to uphold the removal of 'most' of the books and herbarium specimens remaining in Jamaica Plain to Harvard University and declined to pursue the breach-of-trust argument. By that time both the Arboretum and the University had grown more accustomed to working together and the Controversy was over. Blanch died in 1969 with no further action having been taken.

The Controversy had lasted over twenty years, during which time it attracted much publicity, cost both sides an unknown amount, and doubtless resulted in the deferral of needed improvements and investments in the Arboretum's facilities and collections in Jamaica Plain. While Harvard had won the court case, it had been put on notice in a very public way, and it responded with a complete index of the Arboretum collections, and made those taken to Cambridge available for both students and the interested public. The value of the collections became increasingly recognized during this period, and the University ultimately invested in a major botanical facility in Cambridge while simultaneously improving the facilities at the Arboretum.

All of this took place while the Biology Department at Harvard was going through a highly contentious struggle quite apart from the Controversy: James Watson of DNA fame, who had just joined the faculty and who proved to be aggressive and outspoken, strongly advocated emphasizing molecular biology and playing down systematics, including botany, while his colleague, Professor E. O. Wilson, took up the fight on the other side. E. O. Wilson was renowned for his research on the sociobiology of ants, and to keep peace, the decision was made to split the Biology Department into two separate divisions: a Department of Molecular Biology and a Department of Organismic and Evolutionary Biology, the latter being where botany was placed. This separation brought a sense of order that had long been absent, and the conflicts fell away.

McGeorge Bundy was dean of the University in the early 1950s when I was an undergraduate. He later became president of the Ford Foundation, where I was a program officer, and I worked closely with him. He had been involved in the University's response to the Controversy, but never pursued the subject with me. The Department of Organismic and Evolutionary Biology was led by Professor Richard Evans Schultes, who was an ethnobotanist and a successor to Oakes. I took his course, and we later became friends. He never mentioned the Controversy, and he died in 2001. Sadly, E. O. Wilson died just the day after Christmas in 2021, and Professor Paul C. Mangelsdorf had died earlier, in 1989.

In sum, so far as I am aware, none of the principal leaders of the University or the Biology Department are now available to recall or confirm the events of the Controversy. As a consequence, we are left with what can be found in the archives or be gained from the imperfect memories of junior observers, like myself. It is evident, however, that the University now has a strong botanical presence in Cambridge through the Herbaria and Libraries, the Oakes Ames Orchid Herbarium, and the Glass Flowers and Botanical Museum that attracts a constant flow of visitors. The Arnold Arboretum has maintained its invaluable plant collection and acts as an important resource for both students and the public. Perhaps that outcome is in part a legacy of Blanche's remaining a persistent advocate in spite of legal reversals, as well as a reflection of Oakes's botanical research and teaching."

With the Controversy resolved, however imperfectly, and its major players unavailable for further comment, it makes sense to accept Ned Ames's summary and the archival documents as the last words on the matter.

# 9

## The New England Hospital
## for Women and Children

*"For us to compromise on the principle that this Hospital is for women, by women, [and is] to train women would mean complete annihilation in the future and treachery to the founders."*
—BLANCHE AMES AMES

TO UNDERSTAND BLANCHE'S NEXT major challenge requires a brief and highly relevant history lesson as an introduction.

Pioneering doctors Marie Zakrzewska and Elizabeth Blackwell opened the New York Infirmary for Women and Children in 1857. Dr. Marie Zakrzewska moved to Boston to accept a faculty position in obstetrics at the New England Female College. With financial assistance from members of the Board of the college, in 1862 Dr. Zakrzewska, Lucy Goddard, and Ednah D. Cheney opened the New England Hospital for Women and Children, serving a largely immigrant population in the Roxbury section of Boston. The hospital's 1863 charter authorized training of female physicians and nurses and provision of medical care exclusively by female doctors. The first hospital in the entire country to have a nursing school, it graduated the first American-trained nurse, Linda Richards, in 1872, as well as the first Black nurse, Mary Eliza Mahoney, in 1879. It was the first hospital in Boston to offer obstetrics, gynecology, and pediatrics all in one facility and by 1900 was one of the largest hospitals in the city.[1]

By mid-century, however, contrary to the hospital's charter and the wishes of staff and under pressure from its major funder, the United

1. Wall, "Feminism and the New England Hospital," 435.

Community Services of Metropolitan Boston (UCS), the Board had allowed hiring of male physicians, permitted men to be admitted as patients, and closed the school of nursing. The Board officially shortened the institution's name to New England Hospital (NEH) in 1951 to reflect these changes. Worsening the hospital's already shaky financial situation, the UCS threatened to withdraw its support altogether if the hospital deviated from the path of which it approved.

According to Helena Wall's analysis of the hospital's descent into straitened circumstances,

> "Its distinguished past sustained the Hospital's reputation even as its physical plant grew older, its finances more uncertain, its professional attractions fewer. But by World War II these strains showed more clearly, and financial and administrative troubles led the Hospital into a protracted dispute with a major funder, the United Community Services of Metropolitan Boston. The UCS controversy, which began in 1949, opened a debate on the means and ends of women's achievement, a debate which paralleled divisions of thought within the larger feminist movement."[2]

Those two separate though related feminist camps were: the traditional *social* feminists seeking to protect women from discrimination and to consolidate gains already won, and the more extreme *hard-core* feminists seeking to open up equal opportunities for women as individuals and to compete on equal terms with men for advancement.[3] At the same time there was a generational divide, older women on one side and younger women on the other.

According to another account by Virginia Drachman, the hospital that was "born of and nourished by separatism—the nineteenth-century solution to sexual discrimination" was by the early twentieth century confronting "its most formidable challenge: the opportunities of integration . . . such that the fates of the New England Hospital and of the women doctors who worked there were inextricably intertwined."[4] This interpretation attributes the shake-up besetting the hospital to a clash between on the one hand an emerging culture of medical professionalism—whereby institutions of medical charity and service to the community were being replaced by institutions of medical science—and on the other, the long-standing cultures of sexual

2. Wall, "Feminism and the New England Hospital," 435.
3. Wall, "Feminism and the New England Hospital," 435.
4. Drachman, *Hospital With a Heart,* 11.

discrimination and sisterhood that drove pioneering women and their supporters to establish and defend single-sex medical institutions.[5]

Blanche Ames Ames was a supporter of the New England Hospital for Women and Children as early as 1941 when she became a member of the Corporation. When the very survival of the hospital was at stake by mid-century, into the midst of the turmoil strode Blanche, traditional social feminist and staunch defender of the hospital's separatist mission. And where synthesis was called for—the hospital was both a women's institution *and* a medical institution, its doctors both women *and* doctors[6] —Blanche and her compatriots among the lay trustees dichotomized and, as we shall see, ultimately lost the fight.

One of the top doctors at NEH, Margaret Noyes Kleinert,[7] sent a warm, welcoming note to Blanche on December 27, 1950 saying, "What would we do without you?" And she signed it "With love and gratitude, Dyme."[8] (The doctor's use of her nickname, plus the fact that she and Blanche were both born in Lowell, Massachusetts one year apart and both lived past ninety years of age, strongly suggests they were more than mere acquaintances.) But when Blanche joined the hospital Board, the tide had already turned. "The separate world Zakrzewska built at the New England Hospital no longer met the needs of younger women doctors at the turn of the century as they prepared to enter an era of integration in medical training and practice," Drachman noted.[9] And believing that professional equality with men was within reach, younger female doctors began to ignore the all-women's hospital in pursuit of opportunities they perceived to be better. After the founder's death in 1902, the hospital had reluctantly accepted men as patients in an effort to bolster its declining patient population and fill empty beds. Shortening the hospital's name to reflect that change was one thing. Going further, allowing the hospital to hire male doctors, was a clear violation of longstanding hospital policy. Nevertheless, a man was appointed as the new chief of surgery in 1950, and he hastily added more men to the staff so that by the next year fully one third of the active staff were males. These

5. Drachman, *Hospital With a Heart*, 13

6. Drachman, *Hospital With a Heart*, 13.

7. Dr. Margaret Noyes Kleinert (1879–1971) was an otolaryngologist (head and neck surgeon) with a medical degree from the Women's Medical College in Pennsylvania and postgraduate training at the Mass Eye and Ear Infirmary in Boston. Dr. Kleinert, like Blanche Ames Ames, donated her papers to the Schlesinger Library/Radcliffe Institute.

8. Box 1, Folder 10, Schlesinger Library/Radcliffe Institute.

9. Drachman, *Hospital With a Heart*, 200.

actions opened a rift between the staff and hospital administration and between the administration and the trustees. Several of the most prominent female doctors who had been on staff for years resigned in protest. Others, including the hospital's major funder, the United Community Services, saw the changes as a very welcome step.

A special committee appointed by the UCS to study the state of affairs at the hospital recommended that the New England abandon its original charter and become a community hospital, arguing that discrimination against women had lessened so they no longer needed protection and, by extension, separatism.[10] Blanche Ames Ames, a firm believer in the hospital's tradition of separatism by gender as inspired by Dr. Zakrzewska, led the charge against integration with the support of a newly-formed executive committee committed to "carrying on" even though the hospital was almost bankrupt. Their position was stated clearly in a November 9, 1951 letter to Dr. Brown, one of the NEH doctors known to favor integration, in which Blanche, soon to become president of the Board of Directors, protested, "For us to compromise on the principle that this Hospital is for women, by women, [and is] to train women would mean complete annihilation in the future and treachery to the founders."[11] Blanche's letter to Dr. Brown also stated: "If we do not stand by our charter, we have no ground to stand on." The hospital is to " . . . provide for women medical aid of competent physicians of their own sex." She assured Dr. Brown that she had searched her mind to see if her attitude was due to prejudice or "militant feminism" and determined that it was not, since her training and her stand in other causes was always "cooperation, understanding, and equal opportunity." Therefore, she would not compromise.

One month later Blanche had a letter from her brother Del on letterhead of the Institute for Associated Research in Hanover, New Hampshire (where her brother was then working) listing foundations known to give money in the medical field.[12] Blanche used the list her brother provided when she was drafting letters to selected foundations seeking support for the NEH's school of nursing, which had been closed due to lack of funds. She wrote to a Miss Lee, for example, appealing to her feminist inclinations and asking her to make a donation: "The New England Hospital is going through a reorganization after a serious period of decline under

10. Wall, "Feminism and the New England Hospital," 441.
11. Box 1, Folder 10, Schlesinger Library/Radcliffe Institute.
12. December 3, 1951, Box 1, Folder 10, Schlesinger Library/Radcliffe Institute.

the management of a group of men. A new Board of Directors has been elected, with a fine group of women who have for years been interested in the progress of women. We have been fortunate to put the hospital back on a pay-as-we-go basis, but our big problem now is to get our Training School for Nurses re-opened."[13]

At the time, so-called "free-bed funds" were one source of support by which hospitals could raise funds. Contributors could pay five thousand dollars to guarantee a bed, should they ever need it. Although the free-bed funds were kept segregated, Blanche was determined to access them. To do that she needed legal assistance. A friend named LaRue Brown (former acting solicitor general of the United States) and his wife Dorothy recommended a bright, recent Yale Law School graduate named Raymond H. Young. He advised the hospital that the beds could be provided if called for without having to segregate the funds. The NEH could continue to limp along. (Looking back some seventy-one years, Raymond Young remembers Blanche as "quite a character, a fierce lady, a great believer in fighting.")

Despite this satisfying legal victory, the shortage of funds continued to be a major problem, and the UCS was reconsidering its support of the hospital. The secretary of the UCS's Fund Raising Division, Elmer K. Pilsbury, sent a letter to the New England Hospital's public relations adviser Natalie Harris Cabot (Mrs. Hugh Cabot) with stern advice about "putting your house in order." The UCS would approve a campaign of approximately seventy-five thousand dollars for the rehabilitation of hospital facilities. However, it was not to be a public campaign; solicitation had to be limited to people already interested in the hospital and should be conducted between July 1 and December 1, 1953.[14]

A letter from Blanche to Edna Lamprey Stantial, recording secretary for the Executive Committee and one of Blanche's closest advisers, described conflict continuing unabated at the NEH that spring: "Things boil along at the hospital. Miss Dean is pretty constantly under fire and criticism and I guess I come in for my share. I must say I think some of the doctors are pretty emotional and not very logical. It is almost impossible to discuss a proposition on its merits—it takes lots of patience!"[15] (This comment about the difficulty in reasoning with emotional doctors was vintage Blanche, who was appreciated by some and disliked by others

13. February 14, 1953, Box 1, Folder 10, Schlesinger Library/Radcliffe Institute.
14. May 13, 1953, Box 1, Folder 10, Schlesinger Library/Radcliffe Institute.
15. June 27, 1953, Box 1, Folder 10, Schlesinger Library/Radcliffe Institute.

for being an extremely logical thinker.) In an attempt to reduce the boil to a simmer at the NEH, the new Board took decisive steps to remove the public relations adviser Mrs. Cabot, who was considered a troublemaker because she seemed partial to the UCS. Edna Lamprey Stantial was directed to notify Mrs. Cabot that the Board of Directors of the New England Hospital had voted to terminate her for interfering with hospital administration and for unspecified "subversive activities."[16]

These efforts of the new Board were soon foiled, however, by the most serious loss of financing: the United Community Services stopped fundraising altogether for the hospital, allegedly on account of its deteriorating physical plant, loss of patients, and chronic indebtedness. Blanche suspected those were not the real reasons and accused the UCS's leadership of "anti-feminism."[17] On January 4, 1954 Blanche wrote to Mr. Philip H. Theopold, president of the United Community Services, in her capacity as head of the Board admonishing him for the adverse propaganda put out by the UCS or its committees or officials that "has culminated in an anonymous document incorrect in substantial detail and both unfair and damaging to the Hospital and its women patients and staff." By issuing a press release and statements claiming that the New England Hospital has outlived its usefulness, the UCS "reveals a definite anti-feminist bias . . . and strikes directly at the efforts of women . . . to practice medicine on the same basis as that enjoyed by men."[18]

In a subsequent memo handwritten by Blanche on April 24, 1955, we learn that Miss Carolyn K. Winters, executive director of the New England Hospital, was proposing to add more Middlesex men (physicians from an unapproved school) to the so-called *courtesy* staff, and she also wanted the limit on the number of men to be dropped entirely. Miss Winters, Blanche commented, "came into the meeting determined to get her way about these Middlesex men."[19]

By January 1956 Blanche was so alarmed by the internal politics at the hospital that she sent a telegram from Ormond, Florida on the fifteenth of the month to her friend Edna L. Stantial urging her and the Executive Committee not to approve the revised by-laws as submitted. The proposed changes were "too drastic" and the procedure "too hasty."

16. August 17, 1953, Box 1, Folder 10, Schlesinger Library/Radcliffe Institute.

17. Drachman, *Hospital With a Heart*, 192.

18. Box 1, MC-193, Folder 13, Schlesinger Library/Radcliffe Institute.

19. Box 2, M-193, Folder 23, Schlesinger Library/Radcliffe Institute.

No meetings of the Executive Committee or of the Board had been held to evaluate the revisions to the by-laws, and there was an "utter lack of parliamentary procedure concerning the proposals." Of particular concern among the by-law changes were strengthened powers of the president and the executive director of the hospital.[20]

Three days later Blanche had received a legal opinion on the proposed new by-laws from Raymond H. Young. Mr. Young said that he considered the existing by-laws of the hospital perfectly satisfactory and not in need of any substantial revision. The document is "almost preposterously bad," he opined. For one thing, it would silence anyone who might want to ask questions. For another, under the proposed changes, the president, Mrs. George Allen Clapp, would be made all powerful.[21]

On February 21, 1956 Edna L. Stantial wrote to Blanche that "the bomb fell." Mrs. Clapp's confidant and compatriot Miss Winters had requested a three-month's leave of absence to recover from a personal matter, and Katherine Dexter McCormick (Mrs. Stanley McCormick[22]), a Board member and the hospital's greatest benefactor, was angry over the in-fighting surrounding the request.[23]

Later the same year and on a more positive note, Blanche sent a handwritten letter to Edna L. Stantial on Borderland stationary thanking her for the award of merit from the NEH in recognition of her many contributions. Blanche told Edna that she appreciated the citation on the plaque even though "I rather shun publicity."[24] In addition to her organizational work on behalf of the hospital, Blanche was striving mightily to keep the NEH financially solvent. For example, in November 1956 she wrote again from Borderland to tell Edna that she was donating to the hospital the money she had earned for doing a painting. (The painting was of John S. Ames, a cousin of her husband and a leader with Blanche in the ongoing Arnold Arboretum Controversy during the same time period). And, in a larger sense, Blanche was the magnet that attracted donations to the Blanche

20. Box 1, MC-193, Folder 13, Schlesinger Library/Radcliffe Institute.

21. Box 1, MC-193, Folder 13, Schlesinger Library/Radcliffe Institute.

22. Stanley McCormick was the son of Cyrus McCormick and heir to the International Harvester fortune. His wife, a 1904 graduate of MIT, championed enfranchisement of women and was the major funder of the research lab that developed the first contraceptive pill. See: Fields, *Katherine Dexter McCormick*.

23. Box 1, MC-193, Folder 13, Schlesinger Library/Radcliffe Institute.

24. August 18, 1956, Box 1, MC-193, Folder 13, Schlesinger Library/Radcliffe Institute.

Ames Ames Fund for Medical Education of Women, the fund set up in 1956 in her honor and in appreciation for the wonderful service she gave to the hospital. Only the annual interest was to be used for the work, so the capital fund could go on the record of the New England Hospital and be a permanent memorial to Mrs. Ames.

Another bomb fell when Mrs. Stanley McCormick resigned from the Board in December of 1958. Dr. Eliza Melkon informed Blanche and called the resignation "a great tragedy to the Hospital." Mrs. McCormick had given between eighty thousand and one hundred thousand dollars per year for six years to cover the NEH's deficit. She had given fifty thousand dollars for an elevator in the Richards Building. They had now lost all that support, as well as the $1.5 million she would have left in her will to the hospital.[25]

When Blanche replied to Dr. Melkon, she apologized for the unusual delay in writing but she had been kept busy with visiting family members over the holidays. "I have found it hard to turn my thoughts to the tragic situation at the New England Hospital."[26] This may be an indication of Blanche's waning passion for confrontation and change at the hospital as well as a frank assessment of its ever-precarious financial condition.

Solutions for saving the hospital were considered and rejected. Blanche was willing to accept some male doctors as part of the *courtesy* staff (as consultants) but not on the regular *active* staff. She opposed the idea of a merger with another hospital. What she came up with was a publicity campaign to win public support and donations. Drawing on a reservoir of experience from the suffrage movement and the fight to legalize birth control, she proposed two strategies: deployment of speakers to rally support for hewing to the hospital's original charter, and writing newspaper and magazine articles on female patients' preference for female physicians because of their sensitivity and "motherly" qualities.[27] In drawing attention to qualities that supposedly made female physicians especially effective, Blanche risked invoking the so-called "woman's sphere" argument that suffragists had worked so long and so hard to repudiate. Nevertheless, highlighting female patients' preference for female staff became

25. December 4, 1958, Box 1, MC-193, Folder 13, Schlesinger Library/Radcliffe Institute.

26. January 6, 1959, Box 1, MC-193, Folder 13, Schlesinger Library/Radcliffe Institute.

27. Wall, "Feminism and the New England Hospital," 445.

a selling point and a battle cry for the campaign.[28] The intent was to turn the private institutional dispute into a public event,[29] but this time around her publicity campaign failed. In Blanche's opinion it failed because the UCS had exerted undue pressure on influential leaders in the Boston community, newspaper publishers among them.

Things were going no better within the institution where factionalism and ideological differences persisted. Blanche and Edna Stantial gave it their all but were unable to convince younger female doctors that their complacency posed a danger and that they were misguided in thinking they could compete with men on a equal footing. The older women were "utterly frustrated by the task of helping women who didn't think they needed help."[30] Blanche's granddaughter Sarah Plimpton remembers how upset her grandmother was by the situation and how much she cared. And Joanie Ames also remembers her grandmother talking about the hospital fracas and women's rights: Blanche objected, in particular, to male doctors' total power over women's bodies, and she stressed the need for women to have female doctors.

The struggle continued into the late 1950s when Blanche (then eighty years old) and the band of separatism defenders who shared her convictions were "an aging minority at the hospital" with "waning influence."[31] Finally, on December 11, 1959 she submitted a letter of resignation to Mrs. H. Thatcher Spencer, a later president of the New England Hospital Board. The policy of depriving qualified women physicians of the position as chief of the Department of Gynecology and Obstetrics was a breach of trust, her letter explained. Therefore, she could no longer contribute or solicit funds for the hospital.[32]

Somehow the NEH limped along. Without Blanche and her cohort on hand to object, the by-laws were rewritten in 1962 and men were once again permitted to serve on the active staff. Still, the hospital's decline continued unabated until it had to close its doors for good.

Out of the debacle, however, came a very promising solution for the surrounding community when the facility reorganized and reopened as

28. Wall, "Feminism and the New England Hospital," 443.

29. Wall, "Feminism and the New England Hospital," 447.

30. Wall, "Feminism and the New England Hospital," 449.

31. Drachman, *Hospital With a Heart*, 194.

32. December 11, 1959, Box 1 MC-193, Folder 13, Schlesinger Library/Radcliffe Institute.

an outpatient clinic in 1969. It was called the Dimock Community Health Center in honor of Dr. Susan Dimock, a surgeon at the hospital who had died in a shipwreck in 1875 when she was just twenty-eight years of age. According to its website, the Dimock Center now provides over 19,000 people annually with convenient access to high-quality, low-cost health care and human services that might not otherwise be available to its urban community members. Comprehensive, culturally-competent health and community care, behavioral health services, and child and family services are delivered in partnership with Boston's Beth Israel Deaconess Medical Center. The Dimock Center's financial status is secure these days, thanks to foundations, individual donors, and other generous supporters. For example, the TJX Companies has been a partner since 1992, and the Red Sox Foundation, a partner since 2004, has made the Dimock Center one of its five "cornerstone" programs for supporting the health, education, recreation, and social service needs of children and families in Boston. Safe to say, Blanche would have found the outcome acceptable.

# 10

# Conclusion: Still Aiming and Spinning

*"To tell the story of Blanche and Oakes Ames is to intertwine their
legacy with Massachusetts history and the history of America."*
—PAUL CLIFFORD

A S OAKES AGED, HE relinquished most of his various administrative
posts, and in June 1941 he took *emeritus* status and was able to spend
more time vacationing with Blanche in Ormond, Florida where her elderly parents and her sisters had acquired homes. Their daughter Pauline
described the scene in a preface to *Jottings*. The General (Adelbert Ames)
and Mrs. Ames (Blanche Butler Ames) first stayed in an old-fashioned
hotel that was across the street from "'The Casements," a house belonging
to her grandfather's golfing partner, John D. Rockefeller. Then the senior
Ames purchased a house they called "The Whim," located on the mainland near the river, and established the family compound. Oakes seemed
to tolerate being a member of the "In-law Club" at Ormond better than
at Bay View, or maybe it was the winter sunshine and the abundance of
orchid varieties that drew him to Florida.

In a letter dated January 2, 1940, Oakes told his younger daughter
Evelyn that Blanche was mourning the loss of her mother the previous
month with the fortitude expected of an Ames woman: "Your mother is
taking her blow with proper resignation and Ormond seems to be a place
for delightful memories rather than a place in which to nourish a persistent grief. That is as it should be."[1]

1. Ames, O., "Letters to Evelyn." Compiled by grandson Oakes Ames Plimpton. Sent
to author Elizabeth Fideler.

We also learn that he wrote to a colleague, David Fairchild,[2] with whom he shared botanical and museum interests, about his collaboration with Blanche on a book to be called "Drawings of Florida Orchids." There would be sixty-one plates by Blanche with explanatory notes contributed by Oakes. "This little effort is to be a dandy," he enthused. Their joint publication on the orchids of Florida would turn the tables, he hastened to add, by making *her* the senior author.[3]

When in Florida, Oakes also often corresponded with his then graduate student Richard Evans Schultes, who was later to assume his mentor's posts as curator of economic botany and as director of the Harvard Botanical Museum. In response to something Richard Schultes had written to him, on March 4, 1940 Oakes imparted some tongue-in-cheek advice about doctoral work and really awful thesis writing: 1) Find some topic devoid of human interest and make it stupid. 2) Sift out every spark of human interest and write so badly regarding the residue that your ambiguity seems to imply erudition. 3) If you are capable of giving birth to a single worthwhile idea, conceal it. 4) Write a cryptic summary."

On a more serious note, he added that the PhD concentration in systematic biology need not be suffused with provincialism; instead, one should emphasize "the fundamental implications of taxonomy . . . . through their broad application to human affairs."[4] The professor expanded on this theme in a February 2, 1941 letter to Schultes in which he referred to himself as an old man at age sixty-seven and, looking back on half a century of scholarly work at Harvard, compared the prejudices of small-minded men with the great thinkers of biological history whose outstanding qualities were *curiosity* and *an infinite capacity to see the other fellow's point of view*. He concluded with appreciation for the ray of sunshine Schultes's letter brought into his life.[5]

The professor went from addressing his student as "My dear Mr. Schultes" and advising him to improve his vocabulary and written expression by reading from the best English every day—Conrad, Huxley, the New Testament, and Shakespeare—to employing a less formal opening—"My dear Richard." The professor's letter to Schultes of March 30, 1941 alluded to "this horrid World War II" and its impact on civilization and culture. He

2. Botanist David Fairchild had his portrait painted by Blanche.

3. Ames, O., *Jottings of a Harvard Botanist*, 362 and 381.

4. Ames, O., *Jottings of a Harvard Botanist*, 369–370.

5. Ames, O., *Jottings of a Harvard Botanist*, 372.

recommended that his advisee "linger in the realm of research for another year" with the aid of a fellowship. And once again he emphasized the importance of reading the great classics for one's intellectual development:

> "I don't know of any better subject in the botanical field on which to build such a personality than economic botany with its tremendously important human implications and its call for searching investigations among things that really matter. If I were a young man beginning my career all over again, I should try through intensive research in economic botany and ethnobotany to bring more light into the intellectual realm and to take my place, not in a laboratory cubicle, but in the world, and in doing this I would not neglect the duty I owe to my fellow men to be well-read and to be conversant with Homer, Shakespeare, and with the leaders in music and art."[6]

In this passage the professor has distilled his personal ideal of the worthy scientific man, for his mentee's edification and, not incidentally, for anyone reading his *Jottings* in the future.

Nearly eighty years before the term "teaching remotely" became familiar, the professor seems to have succeeded in the art or craft of guiding Richard Schultes through the trials and tribulations of his doctoral studies in Cambridge, Massachusetts while living in Ormond, Florida. Correspondence in April of 1941 reminded his student that "ethno-botany is the link which completes the botanico-anthropological chain," and he should take care in documenting the "treasured traditions" of primitive as well as of advanced cultures lest they "pass from the pages of our experience." The professor reinforced a final lesson about curiosity and seeing the other fellow's point of view with a family story about Alexander Graham Bell trying to interest Oliver Ames III (Oakes's father) and Oliver's cousin Frederick Lothrop Ames in his invention; the cousins deemed it promising as a toy yet lacking any value as "a practical economic contrivance." Oops! The moral: "The crucibles of progress are tended by men with vision. If you tend your crucible with an open mind, with faith in your venture, you may one day find yourself among those who have triumphed."[7]

Another of Oakes's graduate students who also became a highly distinguished botanist was Edgar Anderson. Anderson paid tribute to his mentor

6. Ames, O., *Jottings of a Harvard Botanist*, 372–373.

7. Ames, O., *Jottings of a Harvard Botanist*, 374–375. When these letters were written, a well-educated man like Oakes Ames would not think twice about leaving out *women* with vision who contributed to the crucibles of progress, despite being married to one.

in *Plants, Man, and Life*. In an excerpt from the book that Oakes's daughter Pauline included as an addendum in *Jottings*, Anderson wrote: "Ames had the mind of a scholar with the soul of an artist. Anything he ever did was done to the last trifling detail, but it was done to perfection by his own aristocratic standards and not according to the conventions of his colleagues or his students." When Oakes Ames taught his economic botany course at Harvard's Bussey Institution (the school of horticulture and agriculture adjoining the Arnold Arboretum in Jamaica Plain), Anderson and the other students in the course dismissed it as *un*economic botany, fascinating but useless, whose only real value lay in getting a good grade.

Anderson subsequently learned how very mistaken they all were. The professor's seemingly peculiar research into arrow poisons, fish poisons, balsa wood, obscure fungi, and ancient crops was not "the amateurish enthusiasm of a wealthy dilettante," as some of the students had assumed, but a hardheaded, practical view of plant products as the world's most important natural resources. Unappreciated by cavalier students and scientific colleagues alike, the professor was, Anderson acknowledged, well ahead of his time. For example, in his book *Economic Annuals and Human Cultures*, Oakes Ames mounted biological evidence that anthropological assumptions about early man and the origins of agriculture were way off, asserting that " . . . man, evolving with his food crops, developed horticulture and agriculture in both hemispheres at a time which may well have reached far back into the Pleistocene." Had the professor lived a little longer, Anderson declared, he would have seen "the tide of scientific opinion turning in his favor."[8]

For his fiftieth Harvard reunion in 1948, two years before his passing, Oakes contributed the requisite Summary of his life,[9] a life spent in a society of scholars and in jungles and the botanic gardens of the world. He had found the rewards of scholarship largely in the accomplishments of his students, he said, though he did publish more than three hundred scientific papers in the "unspectacular" field of applied and taxonomic botany and described more than one thousand new species of the orchid family of plants. He could accept being teased by colleagues about his best-selling book—a Glass Flowers pamphlet sold to hundreds of thousands of Botanical Museum visitors—but took genuine pride in uninterrupted demand for his series of books on orchids (the *Orchidaceae*). Honors had come his way

8. Anderson, Addendum, *Jottings of a Harvard Botanist*, 391–392 and 395.
9. Known today as the Class Report and published as the Red Book.

despite determined efforts to avoid the limelight and reluctance to attend professional gatherings. Here he could have mentioned (but did not) receiving the Gold Medal from the American Orchid Society in 1924 and the Centennial Medal of the Massachusetts Horticultural Society in 1929; his election as a fellow of the Linnean Society of London (founded in 1788, the world's oldest active society devoted to natural history), as a fellow of the American Academy of Arts and Sciences, and as a fellow of the American Association for the Advancement of Science; and the honorary doctorate awarded by Washington University in St. Louis in 1938.

With another touch of humor in the Summary, he construed his final Harvard appointment as a *demotion* from director to associate director of the Botanical Museum, one engineered by himself in order to be relieved of administrative responsibilities. As to home life, he was "blessed with a companionable, gifted wife who has been my colleague and playfellow for nearly half a century" and with four "admirable" children. He referenced the couple's joint publication on the orchids of Florida for which his wife was the senior author. (This prompted a colleague to send congratulations on the work, deeming it a "great partnership between man and wife.") With a final flourish, Oakes reminded his fellow alums that botany plays an important part in war, for any shortage of botanical materials poses a threat to the military might of the United States.[10] During World War I he had served on the Botanical Raw Products Committee of the National Research Council. His participation during World War II was non-botanical: he was a volunteer observer for the Army Air Forces Aircraft Warning Service at Ormond on the east coast of Florida and grateful that in a time of national peril he was not "wholly submerged by the backwash of old age."[11] [12]

Many references to war, taxes, politics, and foreign policy were scattered throughout Oakes's letters to daughters Pauline and Evelyn. The Ameses were staunch Republicans, especially Oakes. In a letter to Pauline dated March 12, 1920 he complained that he and Blanche were in New York City getting ready to travel abroad and he was sorely inconvenienced by having to prove his income tax for 1919 had been paid or would be paid in order to leave the country. "This little annoyance is

10. Ames, O., *Jottings of a Harvard Botanist*, 378–382.

11. Ames, O., *Jottings of a Harvard Botanist*, 378–382.

12. During World War I, he helped to identify alternative sources of scarce materials and new uses for raw plant products, and his economic botany students did the same during World War II. Harvard University, www.hollisarchives.lib.harvard.edu.

necessary in order to furnish a host of Democrats with paying jobs," he scoffed. "The sad part of it is that the Government retains, long after there is need of it, the red tape that unusual conditions originated." We get no sense from the extant letters of his feelings about World War I itself, just that it caused the pleasures of travel to be greatly diminished. Perhaps he did speak of the war in entries that Pauline did not select for the book, or perhaps it was less of a preoccupation since his own sons were too young to serve and he was too old for combat.[13]

When it came to the Roosevelt Administration and World War II, it was clear that Oakes had not changed his tune about Democrats in twenty years. He despaired when faced by "the Roosevelt threat" in 1940 and told his daughter Evelyn he would rather be dead than face another four years of the candidate he called "the God-damned Dutchman."[14] In a letter to her dated December 26, 1941 he sneered at what he considered "the aban-donment of our plucky marines on Wake Island" and suggested prowling along the banks of the secluded Tomoka River to see "if by chance the remnants of our Pacific fleet may be hiding there." As to foreign policy, "What better political emetic than our Chamberlainesque Hull or the head-tossing buffoon? Even the Yellow Bellies have superiority in the air [in planes] built with our scrap iron and our gasoline. That is far-sighted foreign policy for you." A few days later he continued to rant: "If Roosevelt can spend a billion dollars a week, then we may look for the worst period in our financial history. The Democrats are past masters in the art of cre-ating trouble. The salvation of the country rests on our ability to throw them out for another half a century."

In a brief digression, he reminded Evelyn that her brother Oliver was still a senior lieutenant, a squadron engineer based at the Naval Air Station in Jacksonville with responsibility for testing all the planes in his squadron and for keeping them flying. The political rant then continued: "What the Demo-crats have done to the Philippines is beyond belief. If we lose the islands, as we now seem bound to do, it will cost thousands in life and treasure to win them back, and until we do that I fear Japan can thumb a big nose at us and treat our fleet with reliable contempt. That's my opinion. You need not adopt it. But when you go back over the history of the American occupation of the

13. Ames, O., *Jottings of a Harvard Botanist*, 315.

14. This letter to his daughter and those that follow are from Oakes Ames's "Letters to Evelyn." Compiled by grandson Oakes Ames Plimpton. Sent to author Elizabeth Fideler.

islands it makes one see red to realize what a mess the Democratic foreign policy has meant in the Pacific. Hell!"

At the end of 1941, he (rather obtusely) reassured his daughter Evelyn in a letter that in a war things usually go on just about as in peacetime except for the rationing of such things as tires, metals and imported foods. His motto: Keep your shirt on and thank God it's no worse. But by the end of May 1942, the inconveniences and complaints were mounting. Plans for him and his wife to fly north from Daytona at the beginning of June had to be scrapped because the nearby Daytona Airport was closing and becoming a military base. He and Blanche would have to go to Jacksonville and fly from there. "This is how the war comes home to those of us who are on the fringes of it," he wrote. They would leave both automobiles in storage for another Ormond season, if, that is, they would be allowed to travel. "Everything we do is spiced with doubts. For a time I leaned strongly toward plans for making Florida our observation post for the duration of the war. I can see horrible difficulties in living in North Easton with all kinds of rationing about us. And the servant problem!" (They couldn't find enough maids.) Of course Blanche was just as inconvenienced by rationing, last-minute changes of plans, and difficulty in finding and keeping household help, but her nature was to make do and deal with the situation instead of moaning about it as her husband was wont to do.

In fact, Blanche was engrossed in perfecting her idea for ensnaring enemy airplanes during bombing raids by jamming their propellers with long, hanging threads suspended from barrage balloons and causing their engines to stall. (See chapter 3.) Oakes mocked Blanche's airplane-jamming project in a January 7, 1941 letter to Evelyn. Devoted as he was to his wife, he could not resist poking fun at her projects. (Her invention of a hexagonal lumber cutter in 1939 may have been one.) In between disquisitions on feeding bread to the ducks and the status of a plum pudding received at Christmas, he said: "Your mother's ever-busy brain is now hard at it trying to dope out some way to overcome the threat of aircraft in wartime. She really takes seriously her recent scheme to fill the air with coiled ropes. She draws queer pictures of rope strands getting tangled up with propellers and rudders. This morning, while still in bed, she wrote a long letter, lavishly illustrated, to Oliver. I tell her that Oliver will advise her to catch her aircraft first and then wind strings round it wherever she sees fit to do so." And he pooh-poohed the project again in an October 16, 1941 letter from Borderland, calling it Blanche's "aircraft destruction hobby" and telling Evelyn that her mother's "unending work on means to destroy aircraft has gone on without interruption."

Blanche had hired a mechanic to live over the garage, and Oakes was put out that the man was spending the daylight hours producing "evil sounds" in the laboratory. New machinery would arrive from time to time, making Oakes wonder how long it would be before every foot of space would be occupied by lathes, drills and electrical gadgets. He described the work outside as more or less spasmodic, then he discovered that it had an unexpected benefit: he could use the new reels adorning the landscape as markers by which to measure his golf shots. Not bothering to mask his cynicism, he joked, "If the aircraft destruction hobby plays itself out in a week or so, we may get off to Ormond before Thanksgiving. Otherwise we may remain here for the duration of the War."

Granddaughter Sarah Plimpton remembers Oakes making critical comments about the politics of his sons-in-law J. P. Davis (the husband of his daughter Evelyn) and Francis T. P. Plimpton (Pauline's husband Francis was Sarah's father), both of whom worked in the War Shipping Administration during the war. Oakes wrote far more approvingly about his son Oliver's service as a navy pilot. Blanche did not leave a similar paper trail, but from William (Bill) Ames's story about his own deployment to Vietnam we know that Blanche followed the news about that war very closely. Bill Ames is a grandson of John Ames, a descendant on Oakes's side of the family. He told me the following story about Blanche, then in her upper eighties, and his posting in Vietnam. When Bill was an intelligence officer at Fort Benning in Georgia, he was assigned to infantry training with a U.S. Army unit headed to Vietnam. He wrote a letter to his grandmother who shared it with her friend, Blanche Ames Ames. Blanche said to Bill's grandmother, "Bring him to tea, I'd love to meet him." Bill did visit and when asked by Blanche where he was going in Vietnam, he admitted that he did not know. She pointed to a map posted on the wall with pins marking certain places and told him, "An Khe in the Central Highlands." Three or four days later, he arrived at his destination, exactly as she had predicted! Bill considered it a good omen, a first-class send-off by the daughter and granddaughter of Civil War generals. (Two years ago Bill found the letter he had written to his grandmother in his parents' files. To this day he regrets not sending Blanche a note to thank her for the good send-off. His chagrin was assuaged somewhat by his involvement in the "Borderland" documentary film project as executive director.)

Threaded throughout Oakes's letters to his daughters are comments on retirement and random thoughts about old age and death. On November 2, 1940 he wrote to Evelyn from North Easton to say that he and her mother had returned from Ecuador and the photos from their trip were all properly arranged in albums. After the news, he continued:

> "With college work more or less over for me I feel pretty footloose, and I could go to Ormond or Timbuktu tomorrow without a single restraining thought. Is it not too bad that retirement and its blessed feeling of freedom is concomitant with old age? It comes at a time when mentality is ebbing and the faculties are dimmed. The only heroic thing about old age is the bluff we put up about it. It is really quite useless for an old man of sixty-six to try to improve his game unless he hopes to play in Heaven. But the mere fact that he tries to do so is symbolic of heroism."

À propos of golf and heroics, granddaughter Joanie Ames savors one family story involving Oakes that was told *to* her some years after it happened. During World War II, her parents Amyas and Evelyn had taken their four children to live temporarily with his parents in Ormond Beach, Florida. Granddaughter Joanie was a baby in a playpen on the lawn. When she saw a beautiful something coming toward her—a venomous coral snake, as it turned out—she reached out her little hand to touch it. Her grandfather, who had just returned from playing golf, saw what was happening, killed the snake with his golf club, and saved Joanie's life. Whether or not Oakes improved his golf game after that, his quick action with a golf club was heroic.

On January 7, 1941 Oakes wrote to Evelyn from Ormond, Florida about the passing of his older sister.

> "For me it was a sad Christmas, and I know it must have been equally so for your mother, because the time in our life has come when we view with consternation the family ranks thinned by death. When Time begins bowling down your alley and comes close to a clean sweep, the single bit of humor in the game is your surprise at having escaped for so many years. We are going to miss your Aunt Evelyn. But the severity of our loss should be lightened by the thought that she was a truly great personality. She was among Ames women 'as bright as a star when only one is shining in the sky.' (I do not have my Wordsworth with me.) However, while family pride is a grand thing, it should, nevertheless, be distributed to the public in carefully measured doses."

Typical of Oakes, his next sentence was about the weather.

From another letter to his daughter Evelyn written nearly five years later and near the official end of the war, Oakes clearly expressed the feeling that time was running out for him. Writing from North Easton on July 22, 1945, Oakes shared a memory from 1916 when World War I "was breaking our hearts." He and Blanche had given their teenaged daughter Pauline a ring, an aquamarine set in platinum, making her younger sister (Evelyn) very jealous. "Little things like this," Oakes confided, "stimulate other memories of very happy times at Borderland. Now, when there is very little room left for me on the lap of the Gods, it is delightful to keep in mind the glorious days of a precious past."

Oakes had a stroke and died eight months later on April 28, 1950 while at Ormond, Florida. He was seventy-six. After his passing, Blanche sculpted an orchid gravestone that she intended as "a monument befitting his life, a memorial to their love of orchids."[15] She began with a design and model in clay of various orchids in panels to be inset on four sides of the rectangular tombstone. A master molder came to Borderland to make a plaster cast of the model which was then shipped to a facility in Long Island, New York where craftsmen of the "lost wax" method could cast her work in bronze. She and Oakes would rest together in a family plot in the Unitarian (Unity) Cemetery in North Easton among the monuments to Oakes's mother and father and grandfather.

Blanche outlived Oakes by nineteen years. During most of this time, "she was still very vigorous . . . she walked [*strode* was more like it] with a wonderful, dignified Boston carriage."[16] Her grandson Ned Ames was visiting Borderland in the 1950s when he was a student at Harvard, and he happened to take a phone call from the North Easton police who had been at the house a few days earlier and were following up to make sure things were all right. It seems that his grandmother, then eighty years of age or thereabouts, was alone in the house when she heard footsteps and called the police. "She readily consented to have them search the house, but *she* would lead the way, pistol firmly in hand." The officer told Ned that he was flabbergasted. (They did discover the culprit: the boyfriend of one of the maids had sneaked in to visit her.)

Ned's sister Olivia Ames Hoblitzelle shared similar impressions: "GrandB moved around that house with a kind of inner power and authority

15. Plimpton, P., "Coda—Orchids in Bronze," *Orchids at Christmas*, 59–60.
16. Clark, *My Dear Mrs. Ames*, 153.

which was really who she was, someone who conveyed mastery of whatever she did." Ever the *doer*, Blanche was heard to pronounce at her eightieth birthday celebration, "Have the courage to act for your beliefs. Whatever it is that you want to do, you can do it. I believe there is no devil but fear."

Pauline A. Plimpton believed her mother was happiest when she was moving water around, building dams to make new ponds, and wielding a shovel along with the men.[17] In a January 27, 1940 letter to Evelyn, Oakes had written with an odd mixture of peevishness and understanding: "Your mother is very, very busy . . . making additions, putting in a newfangled kind of fireplace, all for a decrepit minister from the New York Bowery who is to spend a few months in Florida. I see very little of her during the day as she disappears soon after breakfast to tell masons, plumbers and carpenters how to do their jobs. She stands over them with unexampled pertinacity, and comes to meals dog-tired. This is one method of forgetting your troubles." (Blanche's mother had just passed away.) Naturally, he continued with, "It was too cold yesterday to play golf."

And grandson Ned Ames's story—the one about arriving at Border-land for a visit and finding his grandmother, then age eighty-one, down in an excavation trench in the driveway explaining to the contractors how to wire rebar to reinforce the concrete— confirms the honest but fond appraisals of Blanche we have from Pauline and her father. Ned also remembers an earlier time when his grandmother, then in her mid-seventies, allowed him to use her car, an eight-cylinder Packard, to take his date to a dance at Milton Academy. Normally, her chauffeur Frank drove the big Packard, but when it was time to pick up milk cans from the farm next to Borderland, Blanche would drive and Frank would be in the back seat. Ned realized that she had an unconventional attitude toward work and the servants. "She ran things but didn't lord it over them," as he put it.

Grandson Oakes A. Plimpton has Borderland memories that start with a big snowstorm in 1939 when he was six years old and include the year he lived at his grandmother's house after completing a degree at Harvard Law School. Oakes did not follow in the footsteps of his distinguished father Francis T. P. Plimpton; instead he went his own way by becoming a community organizer and environmental advocate and, in the 1990s, a leader of the "gleaning" movement. Gleaners would pick leftover crops from local farms that might otherwise go to waste and distribute the goods to food pantries and housing projects. He founded and

17. Clark, *My Dear Mrs. Ames*, 211.

managed the Arlington Farmers' Market and oversaw the Waltham Fields Community Farm, both in Massachusetts. "I was born with a trust fund and didn't have to work for a living. I felt I should give back to society," he recently told a *Boston Globe* reporter.[18]

In 1960 when grandson Oakes was living at Borderland, Blanche (then age eighty-two) was for a time running a cattle ranch there, and Oakes helped with the ranch chores. She had ordered a boxcar load of beef cattle from the family's Fort Union Ranch in New Mexico to be shipped east. However, through some confusion at the western end, only cows were sent, so to get calves she needed to bring in a bull every year. The heifers were put through at least one breeding cycle and she subsequently marketed the calves. However, she decided not to continue with ranching and sold off the herd. Oakes also remembers eating TV dinners with his grandmother while watching the news or a baseball game. He claims to have seen Ted Williams' home run in his final major league at-bat. He and GrandB also played pool together. She was "an ace" pool player—she could "aim and spin." And he helped her with research for the book she was writing about her father, Adelbert Ames, whom she believed J.F.K. had unfairly portrayed in *Profiles in Courage*. Grandson Oakes suggested that she focus her writing on the Mississippi years, but she insisted on chronicling the general's entire career.

Grandson Ned Ames shed a bit more light on the cattle ranching story. In his version, Blanche became enthusiastic about the Fort Union Ranch where an exploratory oil well was being drilled on family-owned land in the Turkey Mountains of Mora County, New Mexico. She travelled west with Ned's father (Amyas) and brought with her a small bronze statue of a praying mantis that she placed on top of the well head at the drill site as a good luck charm. The well turned out to contain only carbon dioxide that was then valueless. (Today it would have been piped to Texas for use in pressurized extraction of oil, Ned pointed out.)

Granddaughter Joanie Ames shared this flattering appraisal: "GrandB showed us what it was to be a strong woman." In 1965 Joanie (then age twenty-three) visited her grandmother in Ormond, Florida. "It was simply exciting to be around her, seeing her march along the beach at age eighty-seven. She wanted to show me a nearby cottage she had recently bought and was renovating. As we entered the cottage, the work-men actually saluted her! She walked around, examining all their work,

18. Baskin, "You Might Think Oakes Plimpton Would Live Grandly."

which they knew had to meet her high standards. The confidence with which she conducted herself, her full control of the situation—it was what I expected of a man," Joanie recalled.

To Granddaughter Sarah Plimpton, GrandB was "an amazing character" who was always thinking of new things to do and was always fixing things. "She would read everything (with a pencil). She questioned everything. She didn't accept anything on the surface. She was intent on getting to the truth, the answer." And although GrandB ran the ship of the household and paid attention to the children and grandchildren, it was apparent that she was not confined to the conventional woman's sphere. "Among her people, she stood out," Sarah noted. "She was a social person—certainly in comparison with her husband—and was more independent than the typical women of her time. What made it work was that he supported her and she supported him." They were avid tennis players, enjoyed skeet shooting (she was a very good shot) and playing golf together. If GrandB was less sporty in her sixties and in her seventies when Oakes was gone, she remained adventurous and didn't recoil from anything. Her motto made a lasting impression on Sarah: *Never give up. Always go forward.*

And Blanche did just that throughout her eighth decade. The New England Hospital controversy was grinding on (as discussed in chapter 9) as was the Arnold Arboretum controversy (as discussed in chapter 8). She could take satisfaction in passage of the long-awaited birth control law in Massachusetts and important voting and civil rights legislation at the federal level. The Vietnam War was a growing concern. The environment was as well—she was working on a new invention with her daughter Evelyn, an eco-friendly toilet.

What she turned her attention to, however, was a different problem, one that hit very close to home, literally, because it concerned her father's reputation. John Fitzgerald Kennedy, the junior senator from Massachusetts who was aiming to make a bid for the presidency, had called General Adelbert Ames a carpetbagger in his *Profiles in Courage.* First published in 1956, the book celebrated eight U.S. senators who, in Kennedy's opinion, deserved recognition for their integrity and bravery. However, Blanche objected to a paragraph placed within the profile of Senator Lucius Quintus Cincinnatus Lamar that maligned the governor of Mississippi as a villain during Reconstruction.

Blanche wrote to Kennedy asking for the error to be to corrected whenever the book was to be republished. Weighing in, her grandson George

Plimpton, writer and editor of the *Paris Review* and a close friend of the president's brother Robert Kennedy, met with the president in the White House about the false portrayal of his great-grandfather. When neither entreaty was successful, Blanche saw that she would have to correct the record herself. The title of her book says it all: *Adelbert Ames, 1835–1933: General, Senator, Governor—The Story of His Life and Times and His Integrity as a Soldier and Statesman in the Service of the United States of America Throughout the Civil War and in Mississippi in the Years of Reconstruction.*[19]

Were she still alive, no doubt Blanche would have applauded a 2020 *New Yorker* magazine piece in which Nicholas Lemann questioned Kennedy's reason for selecting Senator Lamar for a laudatory profile when the Mississippi politician was known to be an especially militant secessionist and a defender of slavery. Nicholas Lemann concluded that Lamar must have had an ulterior motive for eulogizing Charles Sumner, the abolitionist Republican senator from Massachusetts who was severely beaten in the Senate chamber by a pro-slavery Democratic congressman from South Carolina wielding a walking cane. Blanche would also have appreciated Lemann's giving her father a central role in his 2020 book on the violent overthrow of Reconstruction by white terrorists in Mississippi in 1875 and its lasting consequences for racial justice:

> "In 1876, Ames was ousted from the governorship of Mississippi after a terrorist-dominated election, which a weary President Ulysses S. Grant, who for years had been far out ahead of the rest of his Administration in supporting Reconstruction, declined to order federal troops to supervise. In 1876, several other Southern states adopted the 'Mississippi Plan' to suppress the Black vote during the Presidential election, and the result was an essentially tied national vote. Lamar, in Kennedy's account, was one of those Southern Democrats who then magnanimously consented to the installing of a Republican President, Rutherford B. Hayes, in return for the removal of federal troops from the South. Lamar's eulogy for Charles Sumner, in other words, was part of a campaign that led to the nullification of the Fourteenth and Fifteenth Amendments in the South and the advent of the Jim Crow era. That is what national reconciliation meant."[20]

And if Blanche were still alive, the bell atop Borderland's roof would be rung for Lemann's provocative conclusion to the *New Yorker* piece, in

19. Ames, B., *Adelbert Ames, 1835-1933: General, Senator, Governor.*
20. Lemann, "J.F.K's 'Profiles in Courage' Has a Racism Problem."

which he asked: "What should we do about 'Profiles in Courage'? It isn't as if the paragraph about Adelbert Ames—who, according to Kennedy, was 'chosen Governor by a majority composed of freed slaves and Radical Republicans, sustained and nourished by Federal bayonets'—is the only one that is problematic today."[21]

Jay Howland (the granddaughter of Blanche's younger sister, Jessie Ames Marshall) had a memorable experience with her great aunt Blanche once while vacationing in Florida with her mother and sisters during spring break. Jay was ten years old in 1952 and remembers Blanche, then seventy-four, vividly. "She was unlike any other elderly woman." Blanche had seen a dead albatross on the beach and needed Jay and her sisters to help her carry it back to the house because it was so big and heavy. Jay remembers the baggy white dress Blanche was wearing and how determined she was. "Once she got a bee in her bonnet, there was no stopping her." Jay didn't know Oakes because he had died two years earlier, but she heard that "it was chilly in the Oakes department."

Grandson Ames Davis has a similar story about Blanche and finding a big bird on the beach in Florida. This one was a seagull, still alive but with a broken wing. The year was 1956. Ames was ten or eleven and had been sent to stay with his grandmother at Ormond to help him recover from bronchitis. ("I had asthma, was kind of shy, and was not an easy child," he said.) He and his grandmother were walking along the beach one day when Ames spotted the injured seagull and tried to capture it so they could take it to the vet. When his hand was badly bitten by the bird, GrandB decided that she would have to capture it, even going into the ocean after it although she was dressed in a linen suit. Her hands were similarly bitten and bloodied, but she did not let go. The vet did what he could and they brought the seagull back to the beachfront house where GrandB's handyman rigged up a cage for it. "I loved that bird," Ames told me, "until the tide came up and drowned the poor creature! What I realized was that nothing could stop my grandmother from what she intended to do. It was an important life lesson. My nature was to be inherently lazy, but she taught me that once you have a goal, you cannot be lazy. Being with GrandB was a life-changing experience for me. She was my surrogate parent."

Ames Davis also often spent time with his grandmother at Borderland while on vacation from boarding school in New Hampshire. "GrandB was in her eighties but definitely not in what was called her dotage; her

21. Lemann, "J.F.K.'s 'Profiles in Courage' Has a Racism Problem."

intellect remained absolutely sharp." She was working on inventions, like an anti-pollution toilet that NASA astronauts might use, and she was writing the book about her father to prove J.F.K.'s *Profiles in Courage* wrong. Looking back, Ames remembers how much he and GrandB enjoyed watching football games on television together and cheering for Johnny Unitas, who was a standout when the Colts played the Giants for the championship in 1959. He and his grandmother played tennis and learned to play chess together, too. "She was very analytical about everything, not just chess moves. I could see that she would figure out what worked or did not work before jumping in—a good lesson for a teenager." Ames thinks his grandmother Blanche was one of the most important people in his life. "An absolutely beautiful woman."

In her ninetieth year, Blanche spearheaded renovation of the Oakes Ames Memorial Hall, which had been a gift to the town from the congressman's three sons in 1881. H. H. Richardson had designed the Main Street building in his signature Romanesque Revival style and Frederick Law Olmsted had designed the landscaping. Blanche was three years older than the structure but in much better shape. The Memorial Hall's roof was badly damaged and the windows were broken. She reminded the selectmen of the town's obligation to maintain the building, put five thousand dollars of her own money toward the repairs, and led the charge to save the Hall. Being Blanche, she climbed up under the eaves with a contractor to make sure he put a layer of tarpaper under the roof to keep out the rain.

Linda Williams is one of the registered nurses who cared for Blanche Ames Ames in her old age. When I contacted Linda Williams about sharing her memories of Borderland and Blanche's last years, she said she would be happy to do it. Of course, she reminded me, as a nurse she would also respect her patient's privacy. To make sure I got the message, Linda told me what transpired when she was approached by the people making the "Borderland" documentary film and was asked to talk about Blanche's personal life: Linda replied that she *could* do that but *would not*.

She told me that three nurses rotated the night shift (11:00 p.m. to 7:00 a.m.) on and off for five years, beginning in 1964. Blanche was not ill all the time. It was "just old age," Linda said. A Dr. Jacobs had sent the nurses to care for Blanche at Borderland. At her insistence, only nurses from Easton would do—Linda Crowley Williams, Pat Hickey Brophy, and Judy Lanigan Baptiste. Linda knew the other women from high school.

Blanche seldom slept when Linda was there. They would often walk and talk during the night, even though Blanche's daughters believed their mother was incapacitated and bedridden. Blanche even took Linda up to her studio on the third floor to show her the drawers of paint tubes and the frame that she used for painting. Linda might draw a bath for Blanche at 2:00 a.m. if that was what Blanche requested. One night, Blanche told Linda that her daughter Evelyn had wanted to be a nurse, but she would not allow it because she had only seen the worst side of nursing during and after the war. Blanche admitted that she later regretted her decision. She told Linda that her two daughters were like night and day. Evelyn was sweet, quiet, and shy, married to a minister (formerly a lawyer) and lived in Nashville, Tennessee. Pauline was the social butterfly who lived in Manhattan. Blanche would point to the large portrait of Pauline at the top of the main staircase and say, "Honest to God. I don't know where I got her!" According to Linda, Pauline's son George Plimpton was Blanche's favorite grandchild. "She was so proud of him and his entrée into the worlds of journalism, sports, and Hollywood. She thought that was wonderful!"

Linda said that Pauline and Evelyn never looked down on their mother's nurses. "The daughters were aware of people's jobs. Blanche and Oakes had raised their children with responsibilities, which was unusual considering the family's wealth and position," Linda commented. (As seen in Oakes's *Jottings* and in reminiscences from several Ames grandchildren, it was no coincidence that both Blanche and Oakes were firm believers in responsibility, in the goal setting, hard work, and persistence that had allowed them and their forebears to prosper across various domains. At the same time, let's be sure to acknowledge that they, their parents, and their grandparents had outsized advantages and resources unavailable to everyday Americans, leaving many otherwise hard-working men and women in the "land of opportunity" to come up far short of their goals.) When Linda worked at Borderland there was a large staff, including a chauffeur, kitchen help, housemaids, and groundskeepers. Blanche or one of the daughters made sure that the kitchen staff would bring Linda hot cocoa and a muffin to eat in the dining room before she left in the mornings. Blanche would order a taxi for Linda and would pay for it.

Both Linda and Blanche loved farm life and agreed that "people come and go, the land is always there, stay with the land." Linda had grown up on a farm in Easton and was raised to be independent. She had free range at a young age and that set the stage for her. Her dad was a Marine and she had four brothers; theirs was a houseful of Irish Catholics. Therefore, one thing that startled Linda was hearing Blanche call Catholics "Black Catholics." Blanche was a Unitarian and a strong-minded person, and Linda was a devout Catholic. She and Blanche agreed to disagree. "We respected each other. Aside from religion, we were on the same page."

That was important, Linda recalled, because Blanche would become impatient with anyone who didn't understand her. Linda told me, "Because of my upbringing, I have a good sense for what is fake and what is real. Blanche was real." She could have six cars in the garage and could attend the theater in Boston, yet she was no snob and did not care for fancy clothes. Her favorite sneakers had holes in them! Linda recalled one night when she found Blanche sitting on the stairs by the library, appearing to be in deep thought. "What do you think about those vases?" she queried Linda. "They are rather ugly," Linda opined. "I agree," said Blanche, "but they're Ming, so what can you do? The problem is, I'm outliving everyone and collecting too much stuff!"

Linda used the word "feisty" to sum up her impressions of Blanche. Whether intentional or not, her use of the word links us back to Blanche's grandfather General Benjamin F. Butler, who was introduced in chapter 1 this way: "the feisty child grew to be a 'fight-some' man, with every obstacle giving him greater determination to win." That was an apt description of Blanche. Nevertheless, by 1969, the nurses knew that Blanche was waiting to die. When Pauline called to tell Linda that Blanche had died, Pauline said she didn't know whether to be happy or sad because her mother had waited so long for this. Like her mother and other family members who preceded her, Blanche did not fear death; she accepted it with fortitude and "died of a determination not to live any longer."

Linda explained to me how she and her family came to live on the Borderland estate. Linda, her husband Jack, and their three young children had been living in Brockton when she was hired to care for Blanche. Blanche had just finished writing the book to vindicate the reputation of her father, General Adelbert Ames. She gave Linda a copy and invited her to read it and tell her if it was good. (This proved to Linda that no matter how high up people go in life, they still want approval.) Linda found the book quite interesting, yet not being a history buff, she passed it along to her husband Jack, who was a high school history teacher with a master's degree in history. Blanche decided to sign the copy to him.

When Linda told Blanche that she and Jack had sold their Brockton house and were going to rent for a year and save up to buy a place in New Hampshire, Blanche offered the use of the empty fourteen-room Tisdale farmhouse where she and Oakes had lived years earlier while Borderland was under construction. With a very reasonable rent ($125/month) the young couple was only too glad to accept. Linda and the children enjoyed walking in the woods and looking for white-tailed deer, foxes, and snakes. She told the children that the woods belonged to the wildlife and the humans were merely visitors to their homes. Her son John loved animals and kept a snake as a pet, carrying it around in his backpack. The Williams family had lived in the farmhouse for barely two years, however, when Jack suddenly died at age thirty-two, leaving Linda a widow with three small children, ages two, five, and seven.

After Blanche died, the three surviving Ames children—Pauline, Evelyn, and Amyas—came to tell Linda that they were selling all of Borderland to the state to be used as a public park. The sale would include the Tisdale property she was renting. However, when they learned that Linda had just recently been widowed, they told her not to think about leaving. "They were such kind people, and they thanked me for the kindness I had shown their mother. Amyas made arrangements for the children and me to remain in the house as long as we needed to." (About five years later, Linda got married again, this time to a "happy bachelor who was not deterred by a widow with three children." Her second husband is also named Jack, she explained with a chuckle, because that way she didn't have to change the towels! She and Jack have six grandchildren and four great-grandchildren. And, once retired from her nursing career, Linda has written books for children, short stories, poetry, and a memoir.)

Borderland did become a state park in 1971, two years after Blanche died. The family had sold the estate to the Commonwealth at a fraction of its real value and donated all the contents of the mansion as well, thus enabling the Commonwealth to preserve the land as well as the unique history of Borderland. True to their parents' vision for the property, it was to be used as a public park, nature preserve, and wildlife sanctuary. To the Ameses' original 1,250 acres the state has since added some 600 more to the park. The Borderland Historic District was placed on the National Register of Historic Places by the U.S. Department of the Interior in 1997.[22]

---

22. Friends of Borderland, www.friendsofborderland.org.

The wise words of Paul Clifford, Borderland State Park's Visitor Service Supervisor for the Massachusetts Department of Conservation and Recreation, capture the significance of Borderland and the lives of its original owners: "To tell the story of Blanche and Oakes Ames is to intertwine their legacy with Massachusetts history and the history of America."[23]

23. Friends of Borderland, www.friendsofborderland.org.

# Epilogue

T HE INTRODUCTION TO THIS biography makes the point that Blanche
Ames Ames was part of women's history for more than half of the
twentieth century and deserved to be better known for that and for other
reasons, that she was someone who was quite interesting and accomplished
but almost unknown, that her name does not appear in history books, that
she was an "influencer," and one who "paid attention" even when attention
was not paid to her. Thus, the reader can imagine this biographer's surprise
and delight upon learning that the new early elementary school in Easton,
Massachusetts is called the Blanche A. Ames Elementary School!

In her March 2020 announcement of the school's namesake, Superintendent of Schools Dr. Lisha Cabral recognized the significant
accomplishments of Blanche Ames Ames. She was Easton's own local
artist, known for her drawings of orchids and contributions to botanical research; inventor of a method to trap the propellers of enemy aircraft during World War II; advocate for the woman suffrage movement;
member of the corporation of the New England Hospital for Women and
Children who helped to raise significant funding to keep it afloat; leader
in civic and charitable affairs; and an author in the last years of her life.
School Committee vice chair and chair of the School Planning Committee
Jacqueline Weisman stressed how important it was that future generations
would learn that Blanche Ames Ames "used her talents to fight for equal
rights for women and to demonstrate that women could be scientists,
engineers, artists and inventors in a time when women did not have the
same opportunities as we do now. Her name has stood the test of time,
and it will continue to do so through the new school."[1]

1. Easton Public Schools, www.easton.k12.ma.us.

Dr. Cabral also explained how the school committee had devised a thoughtful and inclusive process for naming the building. The public was invited to submit nominations that met certain criteria: the chosen person, who had to be deceased for at least five years, would inspire students, would represent local history, and would be relevant to all three of Easton's former K-2 schools. Easton resident Siobhan McKenna, a history teacher in nearby North Attleboro, realized that Blanche Ames Ames fully met the criteria and proposed naming the school after her. "I might have been the person to propose the idea," she told a local newspaper reporter, Donna Whitehead, from the *Journal News Independent* (WickedLocal.com), "but it was Blanche that did all the work."

Indeed, the School Committee voted unanimously in March 2020 to name the school after Blanche. Ms. McKenna's nominee, one of twelve considered by the school committee, was chosen because Blanche's "accomplishments, achievements, and ingenuity spoke for themselves and inspired other members of the community." She was cited as a longtime champion of women's reproductive rights and their right to vote, who led the Birth Control League of Massachusetts, marched with her husband in suffrage parades, drew political cartoons, and organized supporters at her Borderland home. They were equally impressed by her artistic output in multiple formats, by her clever inventions, and by her know-how in managing construction of the Ames Mansion at what is now Borderland State Park where she and Oakes raised their family.

Opening in January 2023 the new building can serve some eight hundred students in pre-K through grade two and 120 teachers and staff. It replaces three aging K-2 schools—Parkview, Center, and Moreau Hall—and is the very first Easton school to be named for a woman. Located at 48 Spooner Street and close to the campuses of the Oliver Ames High School, the Easton Middle School, and the Richard Olmsted Elementary School (for the upper elementary grades), the new state-of-the-art facility houses the Central Office for the school system plus rooms that the general public can also utilize, such as a cafeteria, auditorium, gymnasium, media room, and other meeting spaces. Outdoors, too, multiple playgrounds and sports fields will make the school an attractive hub.

The community of Easton, a town of over twenty-five thousand residents, had voted to authorize the $94.8 million total cost of the project. The district's $59.6 million share of the total required approval of a Proposition 2½ debt exclusion in 2019. Another thirty-six million was contributed by the Massachusetts School Building Authority to cover 55.9 percent of the eligible project costs, those which are deemed educational rather than merely decorative.

Groundbreaking for the project took place in April 2021 at a ceremony attended by many town and state officials and reported in the *Journal News Independent*. U.S. Representative Jake Auchincloss said that Blanche's legacy will inspire the schoolchildren "to leave their mark on the world with the same spirit and passion she embodied." In a similar vein, Superintendent Cabral noted that Blanche was "a leader well before her time." The new school has "spaces for creativity and innovation and civic possibilities, exactly what I believe Blanche Ames would have wanted for our youngest citizens of Easton." Principal Samuel D. Cederbaum referenced Blanche's sense of community and family and envisioned how the new school would "cultivate a garden of learners."

When Phase One was completed in October 2022, Dr. Cabral was pleased to report that the early elementary school project was on target and under budget. In a mid-construction video tour of the school, the superintendent and the principal highlighted a special design feature installed along the curving ramp leading from the first floor to the second level. What the principal called the "centerpiece" of the ramp is an interactive timeline designed to teach schoolchildren, staff, and visitors about Blanche Ames Ames's life. Equally educational is a glass wall through which students can view the boiler room and observe the mechanics of the building. Those features and an "orchid wall" in the cafeteria and a "sensory garden" were bright ideas contributed by several Oliver Ames High School students, then refined and incorporated into the final school plan by the design and architecture firm Perkins Eastman.

In a most curious twist, one of the twelve names proposed for the new early elementary school belonged to Mary Ames Frothingham, a first cousin of Blanche's husband Oakes (and the daughter of his father's cousin Frederick Lothrop Ames). As explained in chapter 5, Mrs. Frothingham was a nationally prominent leader of the *anti*-suffrage movement whose efforts were intended to block everything Blanche and Oakes were working for in Easton, at the state level, and nationally. Beating out her opponent, albeit posthumously, for the honor of having the new school bear her name is a truly delicious win for Blanche! One can imagine her giving the bell atop Borderland a resounding ring to celebrate.

# Bibliography

American Academy of Arts and Sciences. "Professor Ames and Professor Jack of the Arnold Arboretum." *Science 83* no. 2148 (28 February 1936). doi:10.1126/science.83.2148.200.

Ames, Blanche Ames. *Adelbert Ames, 1835–1933: General, Senator, Governor—The Story of His Life and Times and His Integrity as a Soldier and Statesman in the Service of the United States of America Throughout the Civil War and in Mississippi in the Years of Reconstruction.* NY: Argosy-Antiquarian, 1964.

———. (Various dates). Birth Control League of Massachusetts documents; New England Hospital for Women and Children documents. Cambridge, MA: Schlesinger Library/Radcliffe Institute for Advanced Study.

———. "A Grave and Present Danger." *Birth Control Review XV* no. 4 (April 1931).

Ames, Blanche Butler. *Chronicles from the Nineteenth Century: Family Letters of Blanche Butler and Adelbert Ames.* Two volumes, edited by Jessie Ames Marshall. Clinton, MA: Privately published, 1957.

Ames, Oakes. *Economic Annuals and Human Cultures.* Cambridge, MA: Botanical Museums of Harvard University, 1939.

———. *Jottings of a Harvard Botanist (1874-1950).* Pauline Ames Plimpton, ed. Cambridge, MA: Harvard University Press. Introduction by Pauline Ames Plimpton and Foreword by George Plimpton, 1979.

———. *Orchidaceae: Illustrations and Studies of the Family Orchidaceae.* Cambridge, MA: Riverside, 1905.

———. Woman's Rights Collection, Folder 9. Cambridge, MA: Schlesinger Library/Radcliffe Institute for Advanced Study. November 1, 1918.

Ames, Oakes and Blanche. *Orchids at Christmas.* Botanical Museum of Harvard University and Ames Family. Brookline, NH: Hobblebush, 1975, 2007.

Anderson, Edgar. Excerpt from *Plants, Man, and Life.* Addendum to *Jottings of a Harvard Botanist (1874–1950).* Pauline Ames Plimpton, ed. Cambridge, MA: Harvard University Press, 1979.

Arnold Arboretum. 2022 Director's Series. "Birth: The Early History and Meaning of the Arnold Arboretum." (April 11, 2022). www.arboretum.harvard.edu.

———. "Collection Statistics" and "Our History." www.arboretum.harvard.edu.

Arnold Arboretum Library. "The Controversy" Records, 1945-1966: Guide. https://arboretum.harvard.edu/wp-content/uploads/2020/07/1_A_3_2012.pdf.

BIBLIOGRAPHY

Back Bay Houses, www.backbayhouses.org.

Baskin, Kara. "You Might Think Oakes Plimpton Would Live Grandly. You'd Be Wrong." *Boston Globe* (May 14, 2016). www.bostonglobe.com.

Behrens, Roy R. "The Artistic and Scientific Collaboration of Blanche Ames Ames and Adelbert Ames II." Faculty Publications (1998) 4. https://scholarworks.uni.edu/art_facpub/4.

Berenson, Barbara F. *Massachusetts in the Woman Suffrage Movement—Revolutionary Reformers*. Charleston, SC: History, 2018.

Beresford-Kroeger, Diana. *Arboretum America: A Philosophy of the Forest*. Ann Arbor: University of Michigan Press, 2003.

———. *Arboretum Borealis: A Lifeline of the Planet*. Ann Arbor: University of Michigan Press, 2010.

———. *To Speak for the Trees*. Toronto, Canada: Random House, 2019.

Bernstein, Patricia. *Having a Baby: Mothers Tell Their Stories*. NY: Pocket /Simon & Schuster, 1993.

Bessey, Charles E. "Orchidaceae." *Science* 21 no. 542 (May 19, 1905). doi:10.1126/science.21.542.786.

*Boston Evening Transcript*. Sophia Smith Collection, Smith College, Northampton, MA. (September, November 1915).

*Brockton Daily Enterprise*. "Suffragists Hear Maud Wood Park." (January 14, 1915).

Buckley, Cara. "Her Calling: To Restore the Forests." *New York Times* Science Times D1, D4 (March 8, 2022). www.nytimes.com.

Bunting, Bainbridge. *Houses of Boston's Back Bay: An Architectural History, 1840–1917*. Cambridge, MA: Harvard University Press, 1967.

Chambers, Veronica, et al. "Meet the Brave but Overlooked Women of Color Who Fought for the Vote." *New York Times* (July 24, 2020). www.nytimes.com.

Chernow, Ron. *Grant*. NY: Penguin, 2017.

Clark, Anne Biller. *My Dear Mrs. Ames: A Study of the Life of Suffragist Cartoonist and Birth Control Reformer Blanche Ames Ames, 1878–1969*. PhD Diss. Amherst, MA: University of Massachusetts, 1996.

———. *My Dear Mrs. Ames—A Study of Suffragist Cartoonist Blanche Ames Ames*. NY: Peter Lang, 2001.

Crane, Bonnie L. "Blanche Ames: Artist and Activist (1878–1969)." Brockton, MA: Brockton Art Museum/Fuller Memorial, 1982.

Dempsey, Anna. "Women Artists: An Untold Story (1880–1940)." University of Massachusetts/Dartmouth, College of Visual and Performing Arts. (April-May 2015). https://www.umassd.edu/cvpa/departments.

Diamond, Anna. "Fighting for the Vote with Cartoons." *New York Times* (August 14, 2020). www.nytimes.com.

Digby, Anne. "Victorian Values and Women in Public and Private." *Proceedings of the British Academy 78* (1992).

Dillon, Gordon W. "Oakes Ames, Blanche Ames and The American Orchid Society, Inc." In Ames, Oakes and Blanche. *Orchids at Christmas*. Botanical Museum of Harvard University and Ames Family. Brookline, NH: Hobblebush Books, 1975, 2007.

Drachman, Virginia G. *Hospital With a Heart—Women Doctors and the Paradox of Separatism at the New England Hospital, 1862–1969*. Ithaca: Cornell University Press, 1984.

Dubois, Ellen Carol. *Feminism and Suffrage—The Emergence of an Independent Women's Movement in America.* Ithaca, NY: Cornell University Press, 1978.

Easton Public Schools. www.easton.k12.ma.us.

Fideler, Elizabeth F. *Margaret Pearmain Welch (1893-1984): Proper Bostonian, Activist, Pacifist, Reformer, Preservationist.* Eugene, OR: Wipf and Stock, 2017.

Fields, Armond. *Katherine Dexter McCormick: Pioneer for Women's Rights.* Westport, CT: Praeger, 2003.

Flannery, Maura. "Exploring Herbaria and Their Importance." (September-October, 2019). www.herbariumworld.wordpress.com.

Friend, Kevin G. "Borderland—The Life and Times of Blanche Ames Ames." BCN Productions, 2021. www.borderlandthedocumentary.com

Friends of Borderland. "Blanche Ames, Suffrage Leader." www.friendsofborderland.org.

Garay, Leslie A. "The Orchid Herbarium of Oakes Ames." In Ames, Oakes and Blanche. *Orchids at Christmas.* Botanical Museum of Harvard University and Ames Family. Brookline, NH: Hobblebush Books, 1975, 2007.

Gordon, Linda. "The Politics of Birth Control, 1920-1940: The Impact of Professionals." *International Journal of Health Services* 5 no. 2 (April 1, 1975). https://doi.org/10.2190/BFW2-C705-25TE-F99W.

Gordon, Lynn D. *Gender and Higher Education in the Progressive Era.* New Haven, CT: Yale University Press, 1990.

Harvard University. www.hollisarchives.lib.harvard.edu

Harvard University Herbaria and Libraries. www.huh.harvard.edu.

Hay, Ida. *Science in the Pleasure Ground—A History of the Arnold Arboretum.* Boston: Northeastern University Press, 1996.

Heinrich, Will. "Celebrating the Orchid, a Botanical Superstar." *New York Times* (February 17, 2023). www.nytimes.com.

Hoblitzelle, Olivia Ames. *Aging With Wisdom—Reflections, Stories, and Teachings.* Rhinebeck, NY: Monkfish, 2017.

Justia U.S. Law. "Commonwealth vs. Carolyn T. Gardner. Same vs. Lucile Lord-Heinstein. Same vs. Flora Rand. Same vs. Pamelia Ferris." www.law.justia.com.

Kenneally, James J. "Blanche Ames and Woman Suffrage—The Story of the Fight for Passage of the Woman Suffrage Amendment in the Town of Easton and the State of Massachusetts, 1915-1920." North Easton, MA: Friends of Borderland State Park, 1991, 2013.

Kerr, Andrea Moore. *Lucy Stone: Speaking Out for Equality.* New Brunswick, NJ: Rutgers University Press, 1992.

Klein, Maury. *Union Pacific, Volume I, 1862-1893.* Minneapolis: University of Minnesota Press, 1987.

Lemann, Nicholas. "J.F.K.'s 'Profiles in Courage' Has a Racism Problem. What Should We Do About It?" *The New Yorker* (July 23, 2020). www.thenewyorker.com

Leonard, Elizabeth D. *Benjamin Franklin Butler—A Noisy, Fearless Life.* Chapel Hill, NC: University of North Carolina Press, 2022.

Londoño, Ernesto. "VA Is Bringing Back Experimental Therapy Using Psychedelics." *New York Times* (June 26, 2022). www.nytimes.com.

May, Elaine T. *America and the Pill: A History of Promise, Peril, and Liberation.* NY: Basic Books, 2010.

———. "How the Catholic Church Almost Came to Accept Birth Control—in the 1960s." *Washington Post* (February 24, 2012) www.washingtonpost.com.

BIBLIOGRAPHY

McMillan, Sally G. *Lucy Stone: An Unapologetic Life.* NY: Oxford University Press, 2015.
Miller, Heather. "Ames, Blanche Ames (1878–1969)." Harvard Square Library. A Digital Library of Unitarian Universalist Biographies, History, Books, and Media. (July 29, 2012). www.harvardsquarelibrary.org.
Million, Joelle. *Woman's Voice, Woman's Place: Lucy Stone and the Birth of the Woman's Rights Movement.* Santa Barbara, CA: Praeger/ABC-CLIO, 2003.
Moorhead, Joanna. "Melinda Gates Challenges Vatican by Vowing to Improve Contraception." *The Guardian* (July 11, 2012). www.theguardian.com.
Motter, H. L., ed. "Oakes Ames." *International Who's Who in the World.* NY: The International Who's Who (1912). https://books.google.com.
National Park Service. https://www.nps.gov/places/ames.htm.
Noles, James L. Jr. *Twenty-three Minutes to Eternity: The Final Voyage of the Escort Carrier USS Liscome Bay.* Tuscaloosa, AL: University of Alabama Press, 2010.
"On Being." Host Krista Tippett's interview of Archbishop Desmond Tutu. Radio and podcast, 2010. www.OnBeing.org.
Pearson, Lisa E. *Arnold Arboretum.* Charleston, SC: Arcadia, Images of America Series, 2016.
Pierson, Michael D. (2005). "He Helped the Poor and Snubbed the Rich—Benjamin F. Butler, Class Politics in Lowell and New Orleans." *Massachusetts Historical Review 7* (2005). www.lhs-social-studies.weebly.com.
Plimpton, George. Foreword. In Ames, Oakes. *Jottings of a Harvard Botanist (1874–1950).* Pauline Ames Plimpton, ed. Cambridge, MA: Harvard University Press, 1979.
Plimpton, Oakes Ames. *Butler Ames and the Villa Balbianello.* Brookline, NH: Hobblebush, 2009.
Plimpton, Pauline Ames. "Coda—Orchids in Bronze." In Ames, Oakes and Blanche. *Orchids at Christmas.* Botanical Museum of Harvard University and Brookline, NH, 1975, 2007.
————. Introduction to Ames, Oakes. *Jottings of a Harvard Botanist (1874–1950).* Cambridge, MA: Harvard University Press, 1979.
Plotkin, Mark J. "Richard Evans Schultes—Brief Life of a Pioneering Ethno-botanist and Conservationist: 1915–2001." *Harvard Magazine* (July-August 2022) www.harvardmagazine.com.
Pollan, Michael. *How to Change Your Mind.* NY: Penguin Random House, 2018.
————. *This Is Your Mind on Plants.* NY: Penguin Random House, 2021.
Purnell, Sonia. Prologue to *A Woman of No Importance—The Untold Story of the American Spy Who Helped Win World War II.* NY: Gale/Thorndike, 2019.
Roberts, Steven V. *Cokie: A Life Well Lived.* NY: HarperCollins, 2021.
Robey, Harriet Stevens. *Bay View—A Summer Portrait.* Boston: Howland, 1979.
————. *No Luxury of Woe—Reflections on the Legacy of Ben and Sarah Butler.* Boston: Howland, 1992.
Romero-González, Gustavo A. "The Orchid Herbarium of Oakes Ames Today." In Ames, Oakes and Blanche. *Orchids at Christmas.* Botanical Museum of Harvard University and Ames Family. Brookline, NH: Hobblebush, 1975, 2007.
Ruhl, Jan. "Borderland State Park." North Easton, MA. Massachusetts Department of Environmental Management, 2002.
Sanger, Margaret. "The Status of Birth Control: 1938." *The New Republic* (April 20, 1938). www.newrepublic.com.

Schneider, Dorothy and Schneider, Carl J. *American Women in the Progressive Era: 1900–1920*. NY: Facts on File, 1993.

Schultes, Richard E. "Blanche Ames Ames (1878–1969): An Appreciation." Harvard University Botanical Museum Leaflet 22, no. 7. Cambridge, MA: Schlesinger Library/ Radcliffe Institute for Advanced Study, Box 1, 1969.

———. Foreword. In Ames, Oakes and Blanche. *Orchids at Christmas*. Botanical Museum of Harvard University and Ames Family. Brookline, NH: Hobblebush, 1975, 2007.

Sicherman, Barbara, et al, eds. *Notable American Women, The Modern Period—A Biographical Dictionary*. Cambridge, MA: Belknap/Harvard University Press, 1980.

Simpkin, John. "Blanche Ames" (Suffrage/Cartoonists). (September 1997). www.spartacus-educational.com.

Snyder, Laura J. "Blanche Ames—Brief Life of an Intrepid Botanical Illustrator." *Harvard Magazine* (July–August 2017) www.harvardmagazine.com.

Thomas Jr., Robert McG. "Pauline A. Plimpton, 93, Author of Works on Famed Relatives." *New York Times* (April 17, 1995). www.nytimes.com.

U.S. House of Representatives. "History, Art & Archives." www.history.house.gov.

Valentine, Genevieve. "Virginia Hall, The Subject of 'A Woman of No Importance,' Was Anything But." NPR review (April 11, 2019). www.npr.org.

Van Voris, Jacqueline. "Ames, Blanche Ames." *American National Biography*. Oxford University Press (February 2000). https://doi.org/10.1093/anb/9780198606697.article.1500013.

Vassiliki, Betty Smocovitis. "Oakes Ames." *American National Biography*. Oxford University Press (February 2000). https://doi.org/10.1093/anb/9780198606697.article.1300033.

Walecki, Nancy Kathryn. "A Scientific Pleasure Ground—The Arnold Arboretum at 150." *Harvard Magazine* (March-April 2022) www.harvardmagazine.com.

Wall, Helena M. "Feminism and the New England Hospital for Women and Children, 1949–1961." *American Quarterly* 32 no. 4 (Autumn 1980). https://doi.org/10.2307/2712461.

Ware, Susan. *Why They Marched: Untold Stories of the Women Who Fought for the Right to Vote*. Cambridge, MA: Belknap/Harvard University Press, 2019.

Wilson, E. H. *America's Greatest Garden—The Arnold Arboretum*. Boston: Stratford, 1925.

*Woman's Journal* 45 nos. 3, 6, and 8 (January-February, 1914).

*World Biographical Encyclopedia*. "Oakes Ames, Botanist." https.prabook.com.

Yanny, Michael D. "The Shy Yet Elegant Crabapple—'Blanche Ames." Arnold Arboretum *Arnoldia* (1991). http://arnoldia.arboretum.harvard.edu/pdf/articles/1991-51-1the-shy-yet-elegant-crabapple-blanche-ames.pdf.

# About the Author

ELIZABETH F. FIDELER, EdD studied comparative literature in French and Russian at Brandeis University and received a doctorate in administration, planning, and social policy from Harvard University, after which she held senior management and research positions in non-profit organizations. In addition to the biography of Blanche Ames Ames and Oakes Ames, she has written *Margaret Pearmain Welch (1893–1984): Proper Bostonian, Activist, Pacifist, Reformer, Preservationist.*

As a member of the Sloan Research Network on Aging & Work (Boston College), Dr. Fideler focuses her research and writing interests on older workers—mature women and men who choose to continue in the paid work force beyond conventional retirement age. Her books *Women Still at Work: Professionals Over Sixty and On the Job* and *Men Still at Work: Professionals Over Sixty and On the Job* were followed by *Aging, Work, and Retirement* and by the *Rowman & Littlefield Handbook on Aging and Work.* A new volume documenting aspects of an important societal trend will be published as the *Oxford Handbook of Intergenerational Connections* in 2024. Dr. Fideler can be reached at lizpaulfideler@gmail.com and on Facebook and LinkedIn.

# Index